THE ART OF BASKETRY

THE ART OF BASKETRY

KARI LØNNING

STERLING PUBLISHING CO., INC. NEW YORK

A STERLING / CHAPELLE BOOK

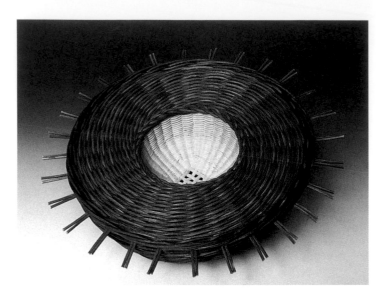

Library of Congress Cataloging-in-Publication Data

Lønning, Kari.
    The art of basketry / Kari Lønning.
        p. cm.
    "A Sterling/Chapelle book."
    ISBN 0-8069-2041-6
    1. Basket making. I Title

TT879.B3 L66 2000
746.41'2--dc21   99-087095

10   9   8   7   6   5   4   3   2   1

Published by Sterling Publishing Company, Inc.
387 Park Avenue South, New York, N.Y. 10016
© 2000 by Chapelle Limited
Distributed in Canada by Sterling Publishing
c/o Canadian Manda Group, One Atlantic Avenue, Suite 105
Toronto, Ontario, Canada M6K 3E7
Distributed in Great Britain and Europe by Cassell PLC
Wellington House, 125 Strand, London WC2R 0BB, England
Distributed in Australia by Capricorn Link (Australia) Pty Ltd.
P.O. Box 6651, Baulkham Hills, Business Centre, NSW 2153, Australia
Printed in China

Sterling ISBN 0-8069-2041-6

For Chapelle Limited
Owner: Jo Packham
Editor: Ann Bear

Staff: Marie Barber, Areta Bingham, Kass Burchett, Rebecca Christensen, Marilyn Goff, Holly Hollingsworth, Susan Jorgensen, Barbara Milburn, Linda Orton, Karmen Quinney, Leslie Ridenour, Cindy Stoeckl, Gina Swapp

Photography: Kari Lønning and contributing photographers
Photo styling: Kari Lønning

If you have any questions or comments, please contact:
Chapelle, Ltd.
P.O. Box 9252
Ogden, UT 84409

(801) 621-2777
Fax (801) 621-2788
chapelle@chapelleltd.com
www.chapelleltd.com

FOREWORD

Each object presented in *The Art of Basketry* is many things at once: a distillation of time-honored traditional basket-making techniques, an innovative reinterpretation of tradition, and a singular personal expression reflecting the unique imagination of its maker.

The artists of basketry presented in this volume consistently devote themselves to an on-going inquiry into the nature of the basket. Through intense thought and effort, they have found unique solutions to self-defined problems of personal expression and, as a result, have distinguished themselves from ancient ethnic and vernacular traditions. This, however, is not to suggest they have summarily dismissed the importance of a solid grounding in the mastery of time-honored techniques. Having educated themselves to a deep understanding of the inherent possibilities, limitations, and appropriateness of various materials, these artists have created extraordinary forms, celebrating an organic unity of concept, technique, and design.

While several makers acknowledge the legacy of traditional hand-woven basketry by incorporating materials which they love and respectfully harvest from nature: rattan, sweet grass, cane, bark, palm husks, others reflect a fascination with 20th century technology by incorporating disparate found industrial materials; paint, photo transfers, acrylics, metal, film, pop rivets, wooden clothespins, and wire. Coupling the traditional and/or contemporary with a myriad of techniques such as wrapping, coiling, plaiting, stitching, twining, embroidery, knotting, and weaving, yields infinitely rich possibilities.

Artists who create baskets tend to use materials that are very linear in character, for example, rattan reeds from nature or copper wires from industry. They are experts at weaving three-dimensional forms, sculptural, functional, or nonfunctional vessels, from linear materials. The ability to conceptualize volume and void is strong evidence of their masterful handling of materials and techniques, not as an end in themselves, but rather in the service of their ideas and desires to create baskets as art.

The objects presented here speak eloquently of the artists' care, feeling, and personal devotion to the making of baskets, which acknowledge the past and most important, bear witness to the time in which they were created.

Baskets no longer need to serve as merely functional vessels, but rather, have become objects that convey the aesthetic values of the individual. Through their work, these artists reveal a strong connection between idea and the final expression of concept. Serving as an inspiration to current and future generations, the baskets featured in this book leave an exquisite and sensitive "record" of the rich, warm, and intimate dialogue between nature, material, and maker.

Michael W. Monroe
Independent Curator

TABLE OF CONTENTS

Detail: "Waterfall"
by Ken Carlson

Detail: "Shadows Cross the Square"
by Maggie Henton

Detail: "Crescent Moon"
by Christine Joy

INTRODUCTION

Basketry is the world's oldest handcraft, and to many, the idea of the "art" of basketry is an oxymoron. Basketry began as a means to gather, carry, and hold food and possessions. But, as we begin a new millennium, basketry has proven itself to be a most creative and diverse art form.

Contemporary baskets have gone from being objective to subjective. The makers themselves define the objects they are bringing to life, pieces which only their own eclectic interests and histories could put together. They are creating dialogues between makers and audiences, ideas, and materials.

Sometimes, this interchange is as direct as a collage of found objects or a personal reverie. Sometimes, it is an ecological challenge to view materials which have been overlooked or discarded by society; or sometimes this dialogue represents a love affair with nature, which culminates in the form of a basket.

Though many contemporary baskets still suggest a vessel form, often these forms no longer have openings or bottoms—they suggest use rather than offer one. As we no longer feel the need to fill baskets with something physical, the contained space becomes as important as the container giving it form.

Now that it is no longer an object's function that defines it as a basket, we look to materials and technique. But even here our expectations have been forced to stretch. Where once willow and oak were the traditional favorites, now clothespins, plywood, and scrap metal are also being used.

With new materials inspiring new work, new techniques are also needed. Once, textile techniques suggested an object's "basketness," but now pieces can be constructed by using wire, nails, or rivets. Where once basket makers used axes and awls, they now have chainsaws, electric drills, and staple guns.

Basket makers, today, come from varied backgrounds. A few have had formal training in traditional basketry techniques, but many began in other fields or out of a desire to work with materials as different as tree bark and sheet copper. For some, the adventure and challenge of inventing their own rules and new techniques were their motivation.

When we are open to the materials and the processes, they become our teachers. With enough experience, our hands and techniques become secondary. But it is only after these basic techniques have been thoroughly learned and pushed beyond the safety of what is known into the unpredictable, that true creativity is born.

Ed Rossback, the father of contemporary basket making, brought up the question whether it is the process or the finished piece which motivates the maker. Clearly this is a balance between the two.

Perhaps if we were all independently wealthy, we would hoard our work and would not be motivated to show or sell it. But, maybe it is the being able to send our work out into the world as a way to share our experience, our realities, and our passions. Maybe it is a way to get people to think about something they had not thought about before or a way to get them to see things from a different perspective. Maybe it is a celebration, a we-do-exist and we have made something for the world to consider, something which was not there before we made it.

My intention for including both how-to and finished work in this book is to show you what goes into beginning a basket, gaining control of the techniques and the materials, developing a design, and then offering you a glimpse into what happens when the

techniques, experience, and inspiration all come together.

I offer this information to basket makers who want to learn how to weave and create, as well as to collectors who want to know more about what work goes into a particular piece. Many of the artists who agreed to work with me on this project photographed significant steps in their design processes. These photographs, along with statements and examples of their finished work will give you a rare glimpse into the evolution of their work and what they have to say about it.

These people have taken their work beyond function and good craftsmanship. They have each developed their own ways of working, their own design solutions, and along the way these basket makers became artists. This book is about the process.

Before You Begin:
A Technical Introduction

The techniques I have described in *The Art of Basketry* are the ones I use. There are reasons why I do things a certain way, but these are not rules. If you find other ways to accomplish the same job and prefer those, then use them. My first basket was motivated by trying to copy the crossed base in a brass tea strainer. I almost got it, but I did not know how to handle the rattan I was using. So I took a basket-weaving workshop taught by Carol Hart. Her enthusiasm and curiosity was contagious. I found myself staying up nights, weaving and unweaving baskets between classes, trying to make them work. That was 24 years ago, and I still stay up nights playing with new ideas and looking for new solutions.

I offer you these techniques as a springboard to get you started. Once you get the basics down, you can build on them. You can go slowly and stop whenever you choose, or go as far as your imagination takes you. Initially this may feel like work, so remember to breathe, relax your hands, and have fun.

Rattan

I choose to work with rattan reed because I can acquire it easily, dye it any color I can think of, work out intricate patterns with skinny strands, and use thicker pieces for heavier jobs. I can depend on its consistency to do whatever I ask of it. Rattan grows in the tropics as a long vine. Seat-caning is derived from the same plant. If you look at the end of a piece of reed, you will see that it contains lots of holes. These are like hollow straws which hold and carry moisture. Before I weave with it, it must be soaked in water to make it flexible. There are differing attitudes as to which temperature is best. I prefer warm to hot water, and recommend three to five minutes of immersion. Since the growing conditions affect its density, the length of time it should stay in water to become flexible will vary. Sometimes strands are so brittle that they just snap, other times they are so tough that they simply will not get flexible and should be used for spokes or larger baskets where they will not have to make sharp bends.

Rattan usually comes in one pound coils or "hanks." It is available in grades, varying from school quality to premium. These grades reflect the flexibility, smoothness, and color. Also available is "smoked" reed, which is chocolate brown in color, and "ultra bleached" reed, which is very white and flexible, but may not be quite

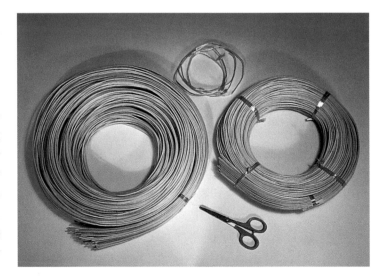

as strong. Rattan is sold in sizes ranging from a #0, which is a very fine 1.25 mm diameter, up to a #11, which is 9 mm; then they continue ½", ⅝", ¾", and up to 1" in diameter. The smaller the number, the smaller the diameter. Generally, I use #3, or 2.25 mm, for weavers and #4, or 2.5 mm–2.75 mm, for spokes. For larger baskets, I will begin the base with a #3, then weave the sides with #4 and use #5 (3.5 mm) for spokes. The #0–#2 can be used for weaving miniatures or for very tight and delicate grids. Keep in mind that the smaller the reed, the longer the weave will take to build up.

I purchase rattan reed in coils for its ease in storage and general handling. Before opening up a coil, I recommend loosening or removing all but the main tie, then soaking the coil in warm to hot water for a few minutes. This helps to relax the tightly wound lengths and makes it much easier to pull out individual strands. I hang the damp reed on a nail over a doorway so I can sort through the lengths. I usually pull out, coil up, and set aside the longest soggy pieces, so that they are available when I need them. When I am ready to begin weaving, I coil up a handful of strands at a time to soak and use as I need them, rather than keeping the entire pound wet. The long pieces are useful when you are working with only one weaver. The shorter pieces are

better when you are working with multiple weavers, since they will not get as tangled up with each other as you work.

Tools

I use only a few, well-chosen tools:

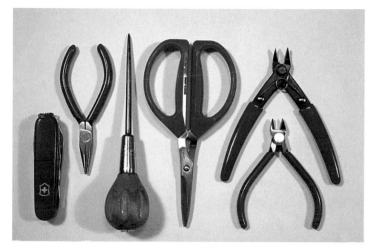

From left to right, top to bottom: Swiss army knife, needle-nose pliers, awl, all-purpose scissors, beveled wire cutters, electrical wire cutters

All purpose, Heavy-duty Scissors — I use scissors which claim to cut anything and which are not too heavy, since I use them all the time. This is important since you want to cut individual weavers as well as the heavier spokes.

Awl — I use an awl with a long shaft, a blunted point and a heavy handle. The long shaft is useful when you need to open up the weave and insert new spokes, because you want these to go at least an inch or two into the base and more into the walls or sides. The blunted point is an important safety feature in case you "get yourself" with it. It is also good if it is not too sharp because you want it to go into the weave, rather than be so sharp that it pierces or splits the reed. The heavy bulbous handle is useful in shaping the final basket.

You can use it as you might a mallet to even out bumps or bulges.

Jackknife — I only use the jackknife for cutting away the backs of spokes in the "grid" base. If your knife is not sharp, you should go find one that is.

Needle-nose Pliers — I use these for crimping. They can be any size that is comfortable to handle.

Yardstick — I find a yardstick is easier to use than a ruler or tape measure.

OPTIONAL TOOLS:

Pipe Lighter — This is not technically necessary, but useful for singeing off the little hairs, or fuzz, which rise from the surface of the reed as you work with it. I use a metal pipe lighter. I do not recommend using disposable plastic lighters because as they heat up; they can melt and fall apart while still lit. Whatever you use, practice first on something less precious than a finished basket.

Small, Beveled Wire Cutters — These are helpful for cutting reed in awkward places, such as inside the rims.

DYES

Since rattan comes already bleached, you can use any dye recommended for cotton, linen, rayon, or silk. I use fiber-reactive dyes, which I purchase in powder form because of their long shelf life. The advantage to this type of dye is that high heat is not necessary to set the color. They also ensure colorfastness to light and water. Use caution when working with fiber-reactive dyes. They are chemicals and should be handled with respect and disposed of properly. Make certain the pots used for dyeing are retired from food use. Follow manufacturer's instructions for disposal.

Manufacturer's instructions for fiber-reactive dye are primarily for use with natural-fiber fabrics. Because there are no instructions specifically for dyeing rattan reed, the following instructions may be used:

1. Soak reed in warm/hot water after loosening all ties so that the coils can soak up first the warm water, then later the dye. Presoaking the reed helps the reed absorb the dye more evenly.

2. Cut all but the main tie. You will need two pots, one 20-quart and one 16-quart. Ease four coils of reed into the 20-quart dye pot.

3. Using the 16-quart dye pot, dissolve two 26-oz. boxes of plain salt and an average of 3 Tbs. of dye for dark colors or 3 tsp. of dye for lighter colors in approximately 14 quarts of water. This will dye 4 lbs. of reed (four coils).

4. Pour the dye solution over the reed in the 20-quart dye pot. Place perforated porcelain plates over the reed to keep it from floating up. Stones or bricks can also be used for this. Let the reed sit in the dye for 12–24 hours.

5. Pour the dye solution back into the 16-quart pot. Mix in and dissolve three cups of washing soda (sodium carbonate). Heat until very warm, but not boiling since the fumes can be toxic. Pour the hot dye back over the reed and wait 12 hours, then rinse.

Rinse by pouring off the dye solution and refilling the pot with fresh water. Continue pouring off water and refilling the pot until the rinse water runs clear. The reed is now ready to use or it can be hung up to dry for future use.

Spokes— How Many & How Long

The easiest way to figure out the length of your spokes is to wrap a long, uncut strand around the outside of something that is approximately the size of the basket you want to make. Allow for 10"–12"

extra at each end for weaving the rim. After cutting the first piece, use it as a guide to cut more.

There is no set formula for figuring how many spokes to use, except experience. You can start with 10 spokes. These will give you a 4"–6"-diameter basket, 14 spokes will give you an 8"-diameter basket, and 20 spokes will give you a 10"-diameter basket. The rule of thumb is to keep the spokes from getting too far apart. Usually, a distance of ¾" is good and up to 1" is all right. If the spokes are too close together, there will not be room for your fingers to hold onto the weave and controlling the basket will become more difficult. If the spokes are too far apart, you will lose some control of the weave and also lose definition in your patterns.

When I begin a basket that will be wider than 10", I start with a 20-spoke base and add extra spokes. For a 15"-diameter basket, I add nineteen extra spokes just before I crimp the bottom and begin weaving up the sides. See Reverse Pattern with 5-rod Wale & Inner Edge Rim Photo 1 on page 37. Spokes can also be added midway into a basket. If the spokes are more than an inch apart, you should add more spokes. The rule is, there are no rules. However, there are recommendations. If you are in the middle of a pattern, adding spokes will change the weave. Sometimes this is very interesting, but sometimes it looks like you made a mistake and did not correct it. I will often weave a band of color to separate and set off the pattern changes. When you make the change obvious, it looks intentional and it becomes a design element instead of looking like a mistake.

In addition to the base, another good place to add spokes or to cut back on spokes is where you make a sharp change in shape. In some of my baskets, I weave a few inches up from the bottom at an angle, then add new spokes, crimp, and come straight up. People look at the shape change, not at a change in the weave.

Weaves

Japanese Weave

After binding your spokes together, you first start weaving with one weaver over two spokes, under one. It will work as long as the number of spoke ends does not equal a multiple of three. Sometimes I use uneven groups of spokes. See Round & "Hairy" with Woven Rim Instruction 2 on page 59. Here there are fourteen spokes, which break down into groups of three and four. Graphically, I prefer to see the larger number group of four on top, but there is no technical reason to do this.

Twining

To twine, you can have any number of spokes and two weavers. See Vertical Pattern with a Twining Band Instruction 5 on page 28 and Square Grid Instruction 3 on page 48. One weaver goes over one spoke, under one, alternate weavers and repeat. Continue weaving, alternating weavers, all around the basket.

If you have an even number of spoke ends and two different colored weavers, the same colored weavers will build up directly above themselves, each row around, creating vertical stripes.

An advantage to twining is that the twining encloses each spoke as you come to it. In the case of starting to weave a grid, holding each spoke as you come to it is structurally important, since holding all the loose spokes in place is quite difficult.

3-rod Wale

As the name implies, the 3-rod wale is woven with three weavers, woven one at a time, one after another each weaving over two spokes, then behind one. The 3-rod wale holds the spokes in place, but also visually covers up the spokes in front as it weaves over two spokes, under one, instead of over one spoke, behind one, as in twining.

You can use any number of spokes, but you will get different results. When you begin with 10 spokes, that gives you 20 spoke ends. Twenty is one less than a multiple of three, so if you weave with three weavers and one less than a multiple of three spoke ends, you will get a spiral pattern. See Spiral Pattern Instruction 5 on page 24.

If you add an extra spoke, the number of spoke ends equals 21, which is a multiple of three. When you weave three weavers with a multiple of three spoke ends, you will end up with a vertical pattern. See Vertical Pattern with a Twining Band Instruction 1 on page 27.

By adding two extra spokes the number of ends becomes 22, which is one more than a multiple of three. With this number of spoke ends, you will get a mottled effect, not spiral, or vertical. See Mottled Pattern Instruction 1 on page 28.

Weaving with one less spoke end than a multiple of weavers for a spiral pattern (20 spoke ends for a 3-rod wale) or spoke ends equaling a multiple of weavers for a vertical pattern (21 spoke ends for a 3-rod wale), also works with 4- and 5-rod wales.

4-ROD WALE

Working with four weavers, you can weave them over three spokes, behind one, or over two spokes, behind two. See Vertical Pattern with 4- & 6-rod Wale Instruction 11 on page 33. The twisting process which occurs when you use two or more weavers, each weaving just one step at a time, strengthens the fabric of the weave.

The base or walls of the basket are further strengthened when you weave behind two spokes rather than just

one and graphically, you cover up the spokes inside the basket. By having more strands woven inside the basket, the walls become stronger. This is especially important in larger baskets.

5-ROD WALE

Working with five weavers, weave the first weaver over three spokes, behind two, then pick the next weaver and repeat over three spokes, behind two, etc. See Reverse Pattern with 5-rod Wale & Inner Edge Rim Instruction 2 on page 37. This is the technique I use most often. It gives me the most design possibilities (five strands of color to leave or change) as well as a very strong structure.

Often I will weave beyond where I think I should stop a pattern or end a basket, just to see what it would look like. More often than not, I keep my experiments.

You can play with the surface height or thickness by increasing the number of weavers you use. As you go from twining to 3-rod wale, to 4-rod wale, to 5-rod wale, and beyond, you will see the reed building up. If you go from a 6-rod wale in one row to twining in the next, the height change becomes dramatic. This can be used in a flat basket or in the side walls. See Round Grid Tray with "Hairy" Sides Instruction 7 on page 56. In the tray, I used all the same color weavers, but you can intensify the height change by using a different color.

TIGHTEN & COMPACT FOR STRENGTH

The importance of weaving tightly varies in different parts of the basket. Initially, you want to weave tightly enough so that each row of weaving rests up against the previous row. In the Japanese Weave on page 14, you take the weaver over two spokes, behind one, then gently pull. You only pull hard enough to affect the over-two/behind-one distance you just wove.

The same short-distance pulling holds true when you work with multiple weavers. Too much pulling can change the shape of your basket. Be careful, especially when your work is flat, such as a tray. The over-two/behind-two/pull will keep the rows of weaving from separating and leaving open spaces. But, if you pull too hard, you may discover that the spokes are beginning to come up into a bowl form.

COMPACT TO CONTROL SHAPE

When a flat base starts to unintentionally round up into a bowl, it may be that your tension is all right, but you need to push the rows more snugly up against the previous ones. Place your left-hand fingers through the spokes and hold onto the basket. With your right hand, hold onto the free spokes and pull with even tension.

Continue all the way around. Begin by tightening every two or three rows, then later in the basket, every four or five rows. Later compacting will help to see if the tension is even. By "compacting" every few rows, you push the rows back up against the earlier weave. Often this will be enough to flatten a tray. However, when you compact a flat base and it becomes wavy or buckles, the earlier weave is probably too loose.

Compacting the bases and sides of a basket should be done every four to six rows. You will not be able to affect or move, more than that number. The exception is with the "hairy" baskets. Since the only thing holding in the hairy pieces is the weaving, you should compact after every row or two to start, then after every two or three rows throughout the basket.

CRIMP & SHAPE

Once I finish weaving a base, I crimp the spokes to make a specific transition. Even when I weave a round-bottomed basket, I crimp so that when I compact the weave, the rows of weaving are pushed back evenly to the same point around the base. Do not pinch and bend in one move as this can break the spoke. If surface cracking occurs, it is all right as long as at least half of the diameter is strong.

The first row of weaving, after you crimp, is the same for all shapes and for any number of spokes. You add whatever number of weavers you plan to use, then weave each strand snugly up against the base. This will require some pulling, but for the most part, it is a mix of "placing" with just enough tension not to have spaces.

The second row is where you start pulling. To get a straight-sided basket, hold the spokes up at a right angle to the base and weave over, behind, then pull just hard enough to make the spokes stand up. Do a complete row of weaving, using the same amount of tension. If you were to continue pulling this hard in the next row, the spokes would start to point in and you would lose the straight sides.

In the third row, pull just hard enough for the weave to maintain an even tension, just hard enough to have the spokes remain pointing straight up. If the spokes begin to flare, you will need to pull a little harder to bring them in line again. After a few rows, remember to compact the weave. This will often tell you if your tension is working.

To weave a rounded bottom, gently pull a little harder in your second row, then again a little harder in your third row. The more dramatic the change in tension, the faster the curve will come up. The less dramatic the change in tension, the more gradual the curve.

If the shape takes too many rows before you see it coming up, it means that you could have been pulling harder. You can either take out a few rows and pull harder earlier or begin pulling harder now. If the weave comes in too fast, hold the spokes out, flaring them a bit and weave a little more loosely than you did in the previous row. Too quick a change in tension will show in the finished basket and could possibly hurt the strength of the wall.

Compacting after a row or two of changed tension will show you whether what you are doing is what you want to happen.

Note: As in the first row after crimping, maintain the same tension for a full row. If you do not, you could end up with a lopsided form. This is all right only if this is what you intended. An easier way to exaggerate one side, rather than with just tension, is to add spokes only to one side or area. The weave will then still be strong, but you can distort the form.

BEGIN & END WEAVERS

When you come to the end of your first weaver, you will have two choices as to where to replace it. There is a general space on either side of the "behind-one." Depending on the length of the end, you will weave it over two spokes, across the first general space, then crimp it just when it comes to the spoke on the far side of this space.

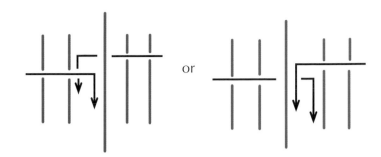

Insert the pointed end next to the spoke you were about to go behind. By cutting the end off at an angle, it will easily slide into the weave. The end should be about ½" long, more if the spokes are more than ¾"–1" apart. You may need to use your awl to open the space a little in order to get the end in next to the spoke. If the end is a bit longer, you can weave over two spokes, behind one, then across that general space to the far side and slide the end in and down next to the far spoke.

The new weaver will begin between the same two spokes as where the old weaver ended, but the new one will begin on the other side of the general space, to the left. The new weaver will overlap the old weaver and continue the pattern as if it were the original weaver. If the weaver ended just after going behind one spoke, but

before going over the next two spokes, the new weaver will be inserted, then immediately go over two spokes.

The right-angle bend, or crimp, is important for visual reasons. Since all the lines in the baskets are either vertical or horizontal, a loose, curving end will draw the eye immediately. Using pliers to crimp your ends is usually only necessary if the reed is very soft or very hard and brittle. Usually, you can just bend the end at a sharp angle with your fingers.

This starting and ending technique, overlapping new and old weavers between spokes, is the same one you use when weaving with two or more weavers. As one weaver comes to the end, you look for the spoke(s) it goes behind. You can end your weaver on the far side of the general space before the "behind- one or two" spoke(s) or on the far side of the general space after you have just gone behind. Replace it with a new weaver as you did above and continue.

To replace weavers when twining, the principal is the same as with three weavers. Take the weaver across the space then slip it down next to a spoke. The new one goes in so that it overlaps the old weaver between spokes then continues the over-one/behind-one weave.

To begin a new color, the process is the same. See

Becoming Band with Double Tapestry Stripes Instruction 3 on page 42. I have woven one natural weaver over three spokes and behind two. On the far side of the second general space, I ended the weaver. On the left side of that general space, I inserted a gray strand. You would end and begin multiple strands of whatever color, in the same way I have changed colors here.

Secure the other end of the very first weaver. If you wait, it may become difficult to get to it. Turn the base over. You will see the end. Cut it off, leaving about ½", or so it is long enough to push under the weaving it is resting against. See below.

POINT OF REFERENCE

The point of reference is the point where you made the

first transition from binding over four or five spokes to under four or five spokes in the base. Use this point of reference whenever you end a base, change colors, or change patterns. When you begin the weavers to come up the sides, or when you are ready to finish your basket, end all your weavers at this point.

By always making changes—shape, color, tension, etc.—at the same point in the basket, and as long as you also compact the weave evenly, you will have even rows of pattern and the height of the sides will also be even. Sometimes a pattern will not end exactly at the point of reference, so get as close as you can and do whatever looks best. If one area builds up a little too much because of making the pattern work, you can probably compact the weave in that area a little more.

As an alternative to turning the entire basket upside down to look for your point of reference, sometimes it is easier to insert a short piece of contrasting reed as a marker. This will allow you to see quickly and easily when you have completed a row. You can also use a marker when you weave "floating" patterns, where you separate rows of pattern weaving with rows of all one color, since it is important to always begin the pattern between the same two spokes.

RIMS

Before beginning any work on finishing the rim, it is important to compact and straighten whatever you can.

The rim will lock in any looseness or height differences that may have escaped your attention until now. Also, it is important to soak your spokes before beginning.

Step 1 — Generally, your choices for weaving off a rim are either behind one spoke, then out, or for a slightly heavier rim, behind two spokes, then out. Weaving behind three spokes, then out, is possible, but it tends to weaken the rim since the reed has to travel so far before it is used. An exception to this might be when the spokes are very heavy or when they are extremely close together. Again, there are few hard and fast rules. I use behind one, then out, when my spokes are getting too short to weave a heavier border, when I want a border that reads as a continuation of the sides or barely looks like it has a rim, or when I am weaving an inner edge. See Reverse Pattern with 5-rod Wale & Inner Edge Rim Instruction 6 on page 38. Going behind two spokes is actually a little easier on the reed and my hands since it does not have to bend as quickly. Also, behind two is stronger than behind one, which is important in larger, wider baskets.

Step 2 — Before deciding how many spokes to go over to insert the ends, do not be afraid of trying different choices for comparison on the same basket. Weaving over two spokes, then in, will give you a minimal edge. Weaving over three, four, or five spokes, then in, is more usual, depending on how heavy an edge you want. The number may vary due to the spacing between the spokes. If they are very close together, you may need to go over more just for technical ease. If the spokes are very far apart or if you are running out of length, you may not be able to go over more than two or three spokes before inserting them.

Note: If you try out different options on the same rim, remember to take out all of the rejected choices before completing the step.

Step 3 — This step is optional, especially for small baskets or for baskets with narrow openings where extra strength is not needed. Also, sometimes the basket opening is so narrow that it is impractical to try to get your fingers inside.

For a light edge or when the spokes are very short, I weave over one spoke, then under. Usually, I weave over two spokes, then under. See Vertical Pattern with 4- & 6-rod Wale Instruction 21 on page 36. For a heavier or a more rolled-edge look, you can weave over three spokes, then under. If you do this or you have already gone around once with over two spokes, then under, and have the extra length, I recommend a second round of weaving over two spokes, then under. This will secure the looser, over three/under row and give extra strength and visual polish to the over two/under row, as well as the over three/under row.

RIM ALTERNATIVES

Another option to weaving a rim is to weave the previous Steps 1–3 inside out. See Square Grid Instructions 15–20 on pages 52–53. This is especially effective on baskets with narrow openings where you want a heavy edge or on a wide open tray form where you do not want the ends to show on the inside.

The woven rim came about by accident. See Round and "Hairy" with Woven Rim Instructions 8–9 on page 61. I was just trying to get all my spokes to flatten out so that I could soak them before weaving off a regular border. As I looped four spokes under the next four spokes, a pattern emerged. I played with it until I found an artistic way to get rid of all the spoke ends. This is one more example of no absolute rules. It also shows how being open to new possibilities can pay off.

FINISH

Once you have finished weaving the basket and its rim or border, there are still a few more steps to take before you stop. First, cut off the excess spokes at an angle so your eye is carried around the edge. When in doubt about the length, intentionally cut a few spokes too long. Step back and look, then cut a little more off as necessary.

Next, rewet the basket and let the excess water drip off. Turn it upside down and push down on the sides until the rim is flat. Turn the basket right side up. Gently encourage it to sit flat. You may have pushed it out of shape a little. Hold onto the rim and gently move it and the sides until it looks even.

If the basket is large enough for you to stand barefoot inside, you can let your toes and heels push up against the curves at the base of the walls. This will flatten the base and even out the base and wall curve. Move your feet carefully around inside, so you do not accidentally kick it out of shape. As your feet are working on the inside bottom, you can gently hold onto the top rim and align the walls to come up evenly around you.

If you notice that one side has a slight bump or bulge, push into it, while supporting the other side of the basket, so that the bulge is absorbed into more of the overall basket, this way it will attract less notice.

The last step is to carefully singe off the fuzziness. Rewet the entire basket. Then, using a lighter, carefully singe off the fuzz.

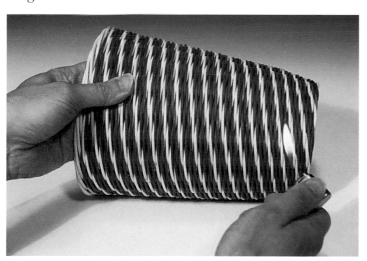

A FEW LAST THOUGHTS

First, my apologies to the left-handed basket makers who are about to read these right-handed directions. I apologize for the inconvenience in having to switch lefts to rights and the far sides to other sides. The truth be known, it is because of your questions that I was motivated to look for new solutions.

Early in my teaching, I wanted to come up with ways to show you how you could weave left-handed. As a result, I came up the with the Reverse pattern/ technique, which is part right-handed and part left-handed weaving. Whenever you see a spiral move up to the left, you can tell that the maker was left-handed, or his or her teacher was. Thank you for your questions. The answers have given me more options, and design possibilities.

Finally, in the pages that follow, I offer you step-by-step instructions to build your knowledge and confidence in using round reed. I have tried to give you a set of basic techniques and a strong foundation on which to build. When I teach, there is always a mixed level of experience. So to create a common foundation and vocabulary, I start everyone out with a 10- or 20-spoke beginning.

For those of you who want to go further, I have given you various design suggestions about how to use these ideas in creating a finished basket. I encourage you to start slowly and be patient with yourself. Then, as you gain confidence and control, I encourage you to take these suggestions and arrange, rearrange, or distort them in order to make the designs your own. Do not be afraid of having to take out something you have just put in. By taking chances, you might just discover the magic and get hooked like I did.

10-SPOKE BASKET

The 10-spoke basket will give basket makers a strong foundation and introduction to many of the techniques which will be used throughout *The Art of Basketry*. You will become familiar with the words I use and how I do things. Being primarily a self-taught artist, I have developed my own ways to start and end weavers, figure out patterns, and how to clean up the basket when I am finished.

The 10-spoke basket is a good place to become familiar with the reed, which pieces to use and where, i.e. use long and very flexible weavers for beginning bases; shorter, stiffer ones for weaving patterns. Here you can practice weaving with three weavers while trying not to get all tangled up in them. (Use different lengths and only one really long one.)

The only technical difference between these three baskets is how many spokes are used. By adding just one or two spokes and doing everything else exactly the same, you can get three different patterns. Here, I offer you three ways to make variations using the same basic techniques.

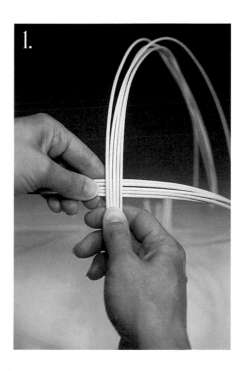

SPIRAL PATTERN

Finished size: 8" height x 6" width

This basket uses approximately 4 oz. of natural and 2 oz. of red #3 reed for weavers, and 4 oz. of natural #4 reed for spokes.

1. Cut 10-spokes, 40" long, then soak them in warm/hot water. Choose a few very long, flexible, natural weavers, coil these up and soak them in warm/hot water. Separate the spokes into two groups of five each and find the centers. Place the midpoint of one group over the midpoint of the second group. This becomes the outside bottom of the base.

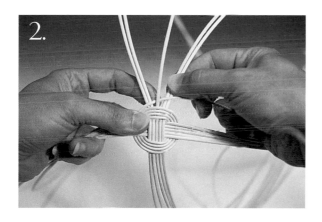

2. With the short end of a natural weaver away from you and to the inside of the basket, bind the top group of five to the bottom group of five by going over the top five, under the bottom five, each four times. As you begin the fifth time around, go over two spokes, under one, then stop. See Japanese Weave on page 14. Check to make certain spokes are centered.

3. As you weave, place your left-hand fingers through the spokes. This helps to keep the spokes equidistant and ensures that the base stays flat. Because it is important to have a strong base from the beginning, weave over two spokes, under one, then pull on the weaver to tighten. Continue weaving until base measures 4" in diameter, then stop and soak the base.

4. Make certain the base is tight and round. Compact the weave. See Compact to Control Shape on page 16. Crimp the spokes to define the edge between bottom and sides. Pinch the reed, using the tip of the pliers, then release and gently bend the spokes up.

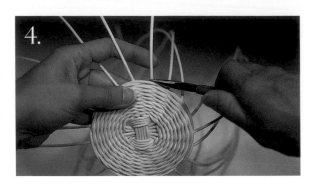

5. To begin weaving the pattern, you will need three weavers. See Begin & End Weavers on pages 17–18. Replace the original natural weaver with a new one, then moving to the right, add two additional red weavers. Add these as if you were replacing old ones. The end of the first red weaver goes in parallel to the spoke to the left of the general space. Repeat with the second new red weaver.

6. To weave with three weavers (3-rod wale), moving to the right, weave the left-most weaver over the other two weavers to the right, over two spokes, behind one, then leave it. For the first row of the pattern, place each weaver securely against the previous row of natural weavers. For the second row, gently pull after going over two spokes, behind one. Replace each weaver as needed as if it were an only weaver. Continue until the basket measures 8" in height.

7. End each weaver over two spokes and end, then compact and tighten the weave evenly all the way around.

8. Loosely loop two spokes behind two spokes, then out. Continue all the way around, threading the last two through the first group. Turn the basket upside down and place it into warm/hot water for a few minutes to soak.

FINISHING THE RIM

9. Step 1 — Undo the loosely looped spokes, then tighten the weave all the way around and even up any unevenness in the height or along the top edge before beginning to weave the rim. Moving to the right, take one spoke behind one, leaving it pointing out. Continue all the way around.

10. When you get around to the beginning, the last standing spoke will thread its way through as if that first spoke were still standing. Use an awl to loosen the first spoke in order to see the space better. All the spokes should be pointing out, or away from the body of the basket.

11. Step 2 — Gently pull one spoke to tighten. Moving to the right, count over three spokes and insert it into the rim just beyond where the third spoke comes out, leaving it pointing in. Continue all the way around.

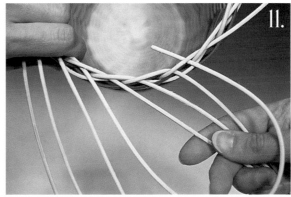

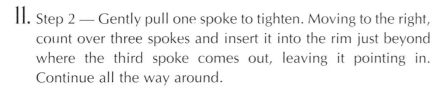

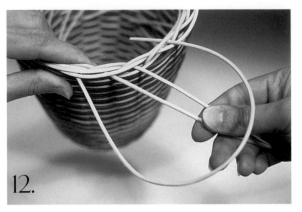

12.

12. When you get around to the beginning, what would be the third spoke is really the first spoke you inserted. Use an awl to loosen this spoke in order to see the space better. All the spokes should be pointing in.

13. **Step 3** — Moving to the right, take one spoke over two spokes, then under one. Continue all the way around.

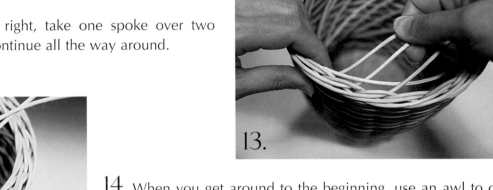

13.

14.

14. When you get around to the beginning, use an awl to open the first over-two spoke and insert the first of the last two spokes. Take it over two spokes (which are woven already so you may need to loosen them), then insert the spoke. Repeat with the last spoke. See Finish on pages 20–21 for final shaping and singeing off any fuzz.

VERTICAL PATTERN WITH A TWINING BAND

Finished size: 8" height x 6" width

This basket uses approximately 4 oz. of natural, 2 oz. of brown and 2 oz. of red #3 reed for weavers and 4 oz. of natural #4 reed for spokes.

1. Follow 10-spoke Basket Spiral Pattern Instructions 1–3 on page 23. The vertical pattern is woven exactly like the spiral. The only difference is the number of spokes. Add one spoke to the existing 20 spoke ends to get to a multiple of three. Do this just before you crimp and begin weaving up the sides. Use an awl to open up the space next to any spoke and insert a pointed new spoke. Soak the base and crimp all the way around.

2. To weave, start with three weavers in three different colors (brown, natural, and red). Two different colors will also work. Moving to the right, weave over two spokes, behind one. When you get to the new added spoke, treat it as if it were any other. By the time you weave the second row, you should see the colors stacking up on themselves. Continue until the basket measures 3¾" in height.

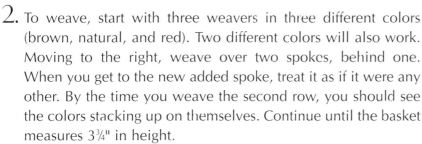

3. Replace the three different colors with all brown weavers by replacing the natural weaver at the same point you inserted the first weaver, then replace the red weaver.

Note: Check the base to see where the first weaver begins.

4. Weave three full rows. Just before beginning the fourth row, end one weaver over two spokes, behind one, then end. Weave the next weaver over two spokes, behind one, then replace it with a natural weaver. Weave the third weaver over two spokes, behind one, then replace it with a natural weaver. You now have two natural weavers.

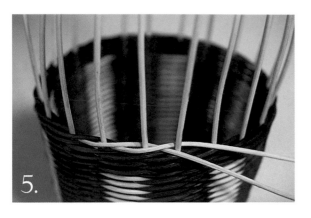

5. To twine, moving to the right, weave the left-most weaver over the other weaver, over one spoke, behind one, leaving it pointing out. Continue weaving, alternating weavers all the way around until basket measures 6¼" in height. Weave three rows, using three brown weavers and one natural weaver, until the basket measures 8" in height. Follow Finishing the Rim Instructions 9–14 on pages 25–26 to finish the rim.

Mottled Pattern

Finished size: 8" height x 6" width

This basket uses approximately 4 oz. of natural, 2 oz. of brown, and one long (9 ft.) red #3 reed for weavers and 4 oz. of natural #4 reed for spokes.

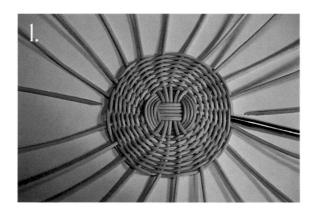

1. Follow Spiral Pattern Instructions 1–3 on page 23. Technically, this is the same 3-rod wale as the spiral pattern. The difference is that two extra spokes must be added instead of one. Add two spokes, soak, crimp, then add three brown weavers. Weave over two spokes, behind one. Continue until the basket measures 4¾" in height. Replace one brown weaver with one natural weaver, then replace the next brown weaver with a red weaver. You now have three different color weavers. Weave 2¼" more in height, then replace the natural and red weavers with brown weavers. Continue weaving until basket measures 8" in height. Follow Finishing the Rim Instructions 9–14 on pages 25–26 to finish the rim.

20-SPOKE BASKET

A brass tea strainer with a double-crossed beginning inspired me to learn how to make baskets. I was intrigued by how the initial pieces were bound together and later how they gracefully flared out to become the skeleton of the basket. That was in 1974. The 20-spoke base is a variation on the tea strainer I studied long ago. It is still the construction I use most often to begin baskets. The initial construction is flexible enough to adapt to specific size needs. Once the base has been woven, additional spokes can be added easily to make wider baskets. Very tall baskets can be woven with a separate base. See Square Grid Instructions 11–14 on pages 51–52. Then long spokes can be added without having to handle the full length of the spokes while trying to bind them together. By playing with the number of spokes and the number of weavers, you can determine what patterns you will get. By "shifting" weavers, or by using tapestry techniques, you can alter patterns even after you thought the number of spokes would dictate getting a spiral or vertical pattern. See Quilt & Quilt, Too with Shifting Patterns Instruction 1 on pages 44–45. By varying the size of weavers you use, or varying the number of those weavers, you can even alter the thickness of the weave.

 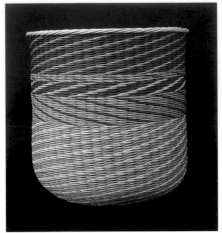 

In the next pages, I introduce more possibilities of designing with patterns. I encourage you to experiment with colors and with mixing patterns. Do not be afraid to try something new for a few rows, just to see what it will look like. You may want to take it all out, but you might be very pleased with what you discover.

Note: My hands are so familiar with the 5-rod wale that I often design a basket first on paper and then work on it as I listen to a book on tape. My hands know what to do from experience, my eyes keep track of the progress, and my mind is free to enjoy the book. This way I can fully enjoy the process and the time it takes to complete a basket.

VERTICAL PATTERN
WITH 4- & 6-ROD WALE

Finished size: 5½" height x 10½" width

This basket uses approximately 4 oz. of natural and 6 oz. of red #3 reed for weavers and 6 oz. of natural #4 reed for spokes.

1. Cut 20 spokes, 40" long, then soak them in warm/hot water. Soak a few long, flexible weavers. Find the center of the spokes. Place one group of five spokes at right angles to a second group of five spokes. Place the third group of five spokes at a diagonal to the first two groups. Add the last group of five spokes at right angles to the third group. You will now have two groups of 10 spokes each—10 on top and 10 underneath.

2. With all the spokes stacked up in your left hand, slip the end of one long, flexible weaver under your thumb. Moving to the right, weave under one under-group, over an over-group, under an under-group, etc. This will bind the over-group of 10 spokes to the under-group of 10 spokes. Continue around two times, then stop.

3. Pull on both ends of the weaver to tighten the beginning. Moving to the left, weave the short end of the weaver in, following the over- and under-groups. When the weaver is too short to weave anymore, leave the short end on the back side or side not facing you. Moving to the right, continue to weave the other end, until you have four full rounds.

4. As you are about to go over the first group for the fifth time, weave over only the first two spokes of that group, then under the remaining three. This becomes the point of reference. Continue weaving over five spokes, under five for the next four rows, weaving over the spokes you previously went under.

Note: This first round should be tight in order to flatten the base. Make certain that there is no slack between rows. Each row should be compacted against the previous row.

5. As you are about to begin the fifth row in the second group of binding, weave over four spokes and under two, disregarding the groups of five. (This is a double Japanese weave.) It is important in the first few rows to compact each row of weaving next to the previous row and to encourage the weave to become round, tight, and flat.

6. In the second and third rows, try and get the spokes to become equidistant. Weave over four, under two, then pull, tightening the last over-four/under-two section. Replace weavers as needed. See Begin & End Weavers on pages 17–18. Continue weaving until base measures 5" in diameter.

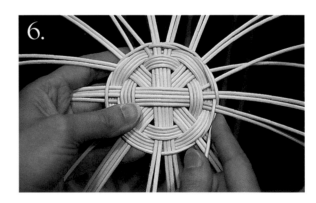

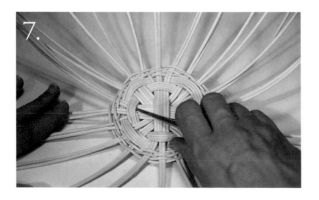

7. Turn the base over and find the short end left over from beginning the binding. Cut the end off to the length of the five spokes it is resting against. Use the side of an awl to push the end under the adjacent binding.

8. When the base measures 5" in diameter, end the weaver you were using for the base at the point of reference. Soak the base. Coil up a few weavers for the sides and place them in the warm/hot water to soak.

Note: When weaving with more than one weaver, use shorter pieces of varying lengths so they do not get tangled up with each other.

9. Turn the base over. Now you will see the outside, bottom of the basket and spokes when before you did not. Use an awl to open a space between each set of spokes, make certain the base looks round. Adjust where necessary, then crimp and bend each spoke gently away from you. Do not bend more than necessary. If a spoke breaks, cut it off at the base's edge, insert a new one, then crimp.

10. Add two natural and two red weavers at the point of reference. It is important to add the red weavers next to each other and the natural weavers next to each other to create wide vertical stripes.

11. To weave with four weavers (4-rod wale), moving to the right, weave the left-most weaver over the other weavers, over two spokes, behind two, leaving it pointing out. Continue weaving until the basket measures 3¼" in height.

Note: In the first row, compact each weaver tightly up against the base. In the second, pull a little harder to begin shaping. See Compact to Control Shape on page 16.

12. End the first natural weaver at the point of reference weaving over two spokes, then replace it with a red weaver. You could also end by going over two, behind two, then replace. Either way is fine, but be consistent. Replace the second natural weaver with a red weaver.

13. Moving to the right, add one more red weaver to the next general space without a weaver ending in it. Pretend you are replacing a weaver with a new weaver. Weave behind two spokes, then out. Repeat with one more red weaver. You will now have a total of six red weavers.

14. Now you are set up to weave a 6-rod wale. Moving to the right, weave the left-most weaver over the other weavers, over four spokes, then behind two spokes, leaving it pointing out. Repeat with each weaver. Continue until the 6-rod wale section measures 2" in height.

15. End each weaver at the point of reference, weaving over four, then end. Loosely loop two spokes behind two spokes, then out. Continue all the way around, threading the last two spokes through the first group. Turn the basket upside down and place it into warm/hot water for a few minutes to soak.

Finishing the Rim

16. **Step 1** — Undo the loosely looped spokes, then tighten the weave all the way around and even up any unevenness in the height or along the top edge before beginning to weave the rim. Moving to the right, take one spoke behind two spokes, leaving it pointing out. Continue all the way around the rim. As you weave, pull gently on the spokes and push down on them so that they lie flat along the top edge of the basket.

17. When you get around to the beginning, loosen the first two spokes in order to see where to thread in the last two spokes.

18. **Step 2** — Gently pull one spoke to tighten. Moving to the right, count over four spokes and insert this spoke into the rim just beyond where the fourth spoke comes out. Continue all the way around.

19. When you get around to the beginning, loosen the first few spokes. Pretend that they are still sticking out. Moving to the right, take one spoke over four spokes, gently pull to tighten, then insert it into the rim just over and beyond where the fourth spoke comes out. Continue all the way around.

20. The last few spokes are a bit tricky to finish. Moving to the right, continue to count over four spokes and insert the end just over and beyond where the fourth spoke comes through the rim, but still in the same space opened up by that spoke.

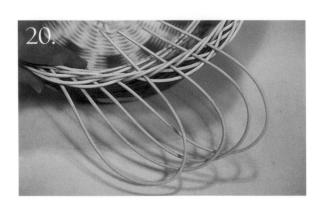

21. Step 3 — Check the rim and make certain that the spokes are evenly tucked in all the way around. Moving to the right, take one spoke over two spokes under one, then leave it pointing out. Continue all the way around the rim. When you get around to the beginning, use an awl to open the first over-two spoke section and insert the first of the last two spokes. Take the last spoke over two spokes (which are woven already so you may need to loosen them), then insert.

22. Step 3 repeated — Weave, over two spokes, under one, then down. This double inside edge gives a wide open shape a stronger, more finished edge. See Finish on pages 20–21 for final shaping and singeing off any fuzz.

REVERSE PATTERN WITH 5-ROD WALE & INNER EDGE RIM

Finished size: 10" height x 15" width

This basket uses approximately 20 oz. of dark grey, 10 oz. of natural, and 3.5 oz. of yellow #3 reed for weavers and 6 oz. of #4 reed for spokes.

1. Follow Vertical Pattern with 4- & 6-rod Wale Instructions 1–9 on pages 31–33. In this basket, 20 spokes are 60" long and 19 added spokes are 27" long. When base measures 5" in diameter, stop and use an awl to open up double spokes. Begin weaving over two spokes, behind one, at the point of reference. See Japanese Weave on page 14. Continue weaving until the base measures 7½" in diameter. Turn the base over.

From here on, the more finished side will point away from you, to the inside. In this photo, the outside bottom is shown with exposed spokes and an awl opening up a space to insert one of the 19 spokes necessary to get a spiral design. To make 19 spokes work evenly, insert one new spoke next to every other spoke, except in two places where you skip two spokes. Place these on opposite sides of the base. Soak the base. Open up the double spokes, make certain the base is round, then, using the pliers, crimp each spoke and gently bend it away from you.

2. After crimping the spokes at the base, insert three grey weavers followed by two natural weavers at the point of reference. To weave with five weavers (5-rod wale), moving to the right, weave one weaver over three spokes, behind two, leaving it pointing out. Continue weaving until basket measures 5½" in height.

3. End one grey weaver at the point of reference over three spokes, behind two. End the first natural weaver over three spokes, behind two. End the second natural and the second grey weavers the same as above. Weave the last grey weaver, over three spokes, then end, before going behind. End two weavers in the same hole. There is no way around it. Use an awl to open up the space.

4. The red reed in the photo is a marker you can use as a point of reference. Since two weavers have already ended in the same hole, moving to the left, insert a new grey weaver just to the left of that next spoke. Add two yellow weavers, then two grey weavers just to the left of the next four spokes.

5. To weave to the left, the left-handers have the advantage. Moving to the left, weave the right-most weaver over four weavers, over three spokes, then behind two. Repeat with each weaver. Notice how the grey weavers build up on themselves, and the yellow weavers build up on the natural to look like an arrow. In the second row, the spiral will grow, moving up to the left. Continue weaving until the basket measures 10" in height. Loosely loop two spokes behind two spokes, then out. Continue all the way around. Thread the last two through the first group. Turn the basket upside down and place it into warm/hot water for a few minutes to soak.

Note: To start and end a weaver while you weave to the left, the basic idea is the same as before. The weaver has to cross the general space and slide in next to the far spoke either just before going behind it, or just before going over the next three .

INNER EDGE RIM

6. **Step 1** — Undo the loosely looped spokes, then tighten the weave all the way around and even up any unevenness in the height or along the top edge before beginning to weave the rim. Moving to the right, take one spoke one behind one spoke. Continue all the way around.

7. **Step 2** — Gently pull one spoke to tighten. Moving to the right, insert this spoke into the rim just beyond where the fourth spoke comes out. Continue all the way around.

Note: Pulling too much will distort the shape. Do not pull the spoke from the inside to tighten since this, too, could distort the rim.

8. If the spokes are still damp, crimp just as the spokes emerge from the outer rim, let go, then bend just enough to point into the center. If spokes have dried, soak for a few minutes.

9. Begin a 4-rod wale by placing the ends of four weavers under four consecutive spokes and moving to the right, weave over two spokes, then under two. Hold the spokes pointing toward the center and compact the weaving tightly against the rim. Do not pull too hard or the weave will come away from the edges. Continue weaving for five complete rows.

10. Weave each weaver over two spokes, then end. Tighten and compact the weave. If the spokes have dried, soak in warm/hot water for a few minutes.

Note: The inner core may still be wet and flexible even if the surface feels dry.

Step 1 — Moving to the right, take one spoke under two spokes, then up. Continue all the way around.

11. Step 2 — Gently, tighten one spoke. Count over two spokes, then thread the tightened spoke just beyond and over the second spoke in the same space it came out of, leaving the spoke pointing into the bottom of the basket. Continue all the way around. When you get around to the beginning, use an awl to loosen the first spokes in order to see where to thread in the last two spokes. Follow Finishing the Rim Step 3 Instructions 21–22 on page 36.

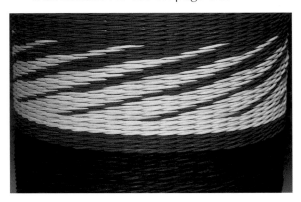

BECOMING

Becoming: having one color blend into another.

Finished size: 11½" height x 12" width

This basket uses approximately 1 lb. dark grey, a scant 1 lb. blue, and 4 oz. natural of #3 reed for weavers and 6 oz. natural of #4 reed for spokes.

1. Follow Vertical Pattern with 4- & 6-rod Wale Instructions 1–6 on pages 31–32. In this basket, 20 spokes are 54" long and 14 added spokes are 24" long. Weave until base measures 7" in diameter. Soak, then crimp. Add five grey weavers and weave over three spokes, behind two at a 45° angle. See 5-rod Wale on page 15. Continue weaving until basket measures 12" in diameter. Add the 14 new spokes. (This makes one less than a multiple of five spoke ends for a spiral pattern.) Soak, crimp, then weave straight up until the basket measures 6" in height. Replace the five grey weavers with five blue weavers at the point of reference. See Becoming Band with Double Tapestry Stripes Photo 3 on page 42. Weave five rows, then replace the five blue weavers with four natural weavers. Weave three rows. Replace one natural weaver with one blue at the point of reference, and weave four rows. As you begin the fifth row, add a second blue weaver. The blue weaver replaces the natural weaver that comes immediately after weaving the first blue over three spokes, behind two, then out. Weave four rows with two blue weavers. As you begin the fifth row, replace the third natural weaver with a blue weaver.

40

2. Weave three rows with three blue weavers, then replace the fourth natural weaver with a fourth blue weaver. Weave three more rows. Finally, replace the last natural weaver with a blue weaver. To balance the natural weavers you used earlier, weave eight rows with five blue weavers.

Loosely loop two spokes behind two, then out. Continue all the way around, threading the last two through the first group. Turn the basket upside down and place it into warm/hot water for a few minutes to soak. Follow Finishing the Rim Instructions 16–22 on pages 35–36.

Note: Notice how the color of the spokes is tied into the colors and overall design of the basket.

BECOMING BAND WITH DOUBLE TAPESTRY STRIPES

Finished size: 12" height x 14" width

This basket uses approximately 1 lb. 4 oz. natural, 6 oz. purple, 6 oz. taupe, and several dark grey of #3 reed for weavers and 6 oz. natural of #4 reed for spokes.

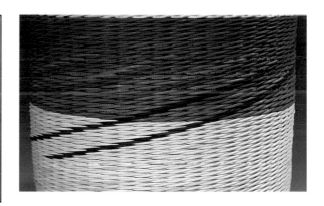

1. Follow Becoming Instruction 1 on page 40. Weave up the walls with five natural weavers until the basket measures 4½" in height. Replace one natural weaver with a short grey weaver at the point of reference. Weave the grey weaver over three spokes, behind two, then out. Weave the remaining natural weavers until you get to the grey weaver. Weave the short grey weaver over three spokes, behind two, then end.

2. Replace the grey with a natural weaver. You now have five natural weavers. Continue weaving until you come around to the tapestry area. Begin the grey in the general space just to the right of the one in the previous row. This will make the grey spiral up to the right. Continue weaving until basket measures 6" in height.

Note: Follow Instruction 2 above whenever you come to the tapestry areas. Replace whatever color weaver that comes through the general space just to the right of where the tapestry began in the previous row with a grey weaver. Continue weaving the double tapestry stripes through the becoming band, disregarding the becoming pattern.

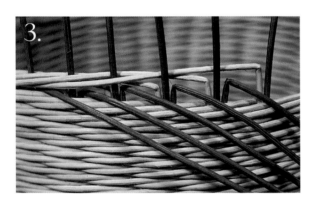

3. Replace each natural weaver with a taupe weaver at the point of reference, until you have five consecutive taupe weavers. Weave a 5-rod wale, over three spokes, behind two, then out. Continue weaving for three rows, then stop.

4. On this basket, the taupe will become purple in only a few inches. Replace the first taupe weaver with a purple weaver, then weave three rows. Replace the second taupe weaver with a purple weaver, then weave three rows. Replace the third taupe weaver with a purple weaver, then weave three rows. Replace the fourth taupe weaver with a purple weaver, then weave four rows. Replace the fifth taupe weaver with a purple weaver, then weave eight rows with all purple weavers.

5. Replace each purple weaver with a natural weaver at the point of reference, until you have five consecutive natural weavers. Continue weaving for five rows, then end each natural weaver at the point of reference. Loosely loop two spokes behind two, then out. Continue all the way around, threading the last two through the first group. Turn the basket upside down and place it into warm/hot water for a few minutes to soak. Follow Finishing the Rim Instructions 16–22 on pages 35–36.

BECOMING WITH BROKEN TAPESTRY

Finished size: 10" height x 15" width

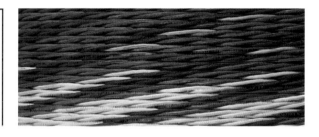

1. To weave this becoming pattern, weave with a 5-rod wale. Replace one natural weaver with a red weaver and weave for two rows. Replace a second natural weaver with an orange weaver and weave for two rows. Replace the orange weaver with a second red weaver. Replace the next natural weaver with the orange weaver, then weave for two rows. Replace the next natural weaver with an orange weaver, weave for two rows, and repeat this step with the last natural weaver. For the tapestry technique, skip a row between adding tapestry. The spiral makes it easy to keep track of moving over two general spaces. Add the yellow weaver just after the second red weaver, replacing the orange weaver for a short distance each time around.

GREENHOUSE SERIES 9, STACKED TAPESTRY

Finished size: 21" height x 24" width

1. This basket is an example of using the tapestry technique stacked up at the same point in the basket. Starting and ending is done between the same spokes as you weave upward with a 5-rod wale. Instead of replacing one weaver, three consecutive weavers are replaced. Weave each over three spokes, behind two, then replace each weaver with a short dark grey weaver each round.

Note: It can be difficult to start and end so many weavers in the same spaces. You may want to skip a row in between adding tapestry. For interest, you can also weave blocks of tapestry where you weave the tapestry stacked for a few rows. Skip a few rows, then repeat weaving the tapestry.

QUILT & QUILT, TOO WITH SHIFTING PATTERNS

Finished size: 15" height x 14" width

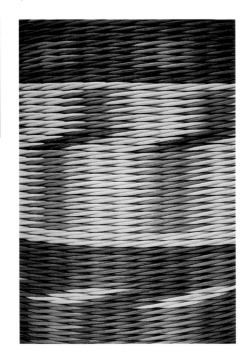

1. This basket is woven with a multiple of five spoke ends (i.e. 20 spokes plus 15 added spokes makes 55 spoke ends) and five weavers, so a vertical pattern will happen naturally. After weaving a few rows with two peach weavers and three green weavers, replace both peach weavers with natural weavers for one row. In the second row, replace the first natural weaver with a green weaver, skip the second natural weaver, then replace the next green weaver with a natural weaver. This maintains two natural weavers, but shifts the pattern one step to the right. In the third row, repeat what you did in the previous row.

1.

After weaving three rows with shifting natural weavers, replace the two natural weavers with two lavender weavers, then continue to weave, letting the lavender and green pattern build up vertically. In the upper area where natural is the background color, repeat the vertical pattern with peach and lavender weavers, then use green weavers to create the shifting pattern.

Note: The detailed photograph above and the full basket photo to the right are two baskets that are variations of each other. The shifting technique adds movement and interest to a vertical pattern.

Storm Clouds with Floating Patterns

Finished size: 12" height x 14½" width

1.

1. This floating effect is achieved by weaving a 5-rod wale in multiple rows of pattern separated by two rows of background color. By increasing the number of dark grey weavers in the upper patterns, the clouds appear to grow more ominous.

THE GRID

In a 1979 article for *American Craft Magazine*, Betty Park wrote, "Baskets register the essence of textile structure—the skeleton of warp and weft." The grid construction represents basketry in its purest sense.

At one time, I thought I wanted to be an architect. Instead I went on to study textiles and weaving. The grid offers me a way to weave and to build. I can play with weaving techniques while building structures. Often I construct grids as open "floors" which I use in double-wall constructions. These allow the observer a partial look into the void, the space which is enclosed between the outer and inner baskets.

The grid is a versatile construction. It can be woven into square, rectangular, or triangular forms. Tapestry techniques can be used either to maintain these forms or can be used to transform them into other shapes. I often begin a square grid knowing that I will turn it into the circular base for one of my double-wall constructions or open trays. The tray lends itself well to showcasing the grid's potential. Grids can be woven with single or double elements, in dyed or natural reed.

By building up the number of weavers, i.e. progressively going from two weavers to six weavers, mountains and valleys can grow and appear to be rippling away from the center point as shown in Round Tray with "Hairy" Sides on page 54. The side walls of these trays can be woven with texture or patterns of their own or treated as frames to highlight the earlier work.

Grids take so long to prepare, construct, and weave that you have more than adequate time to think about what you want to do. Sometimes you can get quite carried away in your thoughts. Other times it is simply peaceful to enjoy the process and listen to the birds and leaves.

Square Grid

Finished size: 5½" height x 7¼" width

This basket uses approximately 4 oz. of natural and 4 oz. of dark grey #3 reed for weavers and 2 oz. of natural #4 reed for spokes.

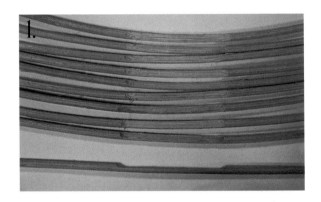

1. Cut 10 spokes, 12" long, then soak them in warm/hot water. Coil up and soak a few very long weavers. Use a pencil to mark a 2" section in the center of one spoke. Cut away just less than half the thickness of this 2" area. Use this spoke to measure and mark the other spokes, then cut these spokes as you did the first.

2. Start with three parallel soaked spokes perpendicular to you as you work on a flat surface. Weave the first cross-spoke over, under, over, centering it on the vertical spokes. Weave the second cross-spoke above the first, then the third cross-spoke below the first, weaving under, over, under. Center these six spokes, then add one extra spoke to each side, weaving over or under to make the pattern work. You should now have five vertical and five horizontal spokes.

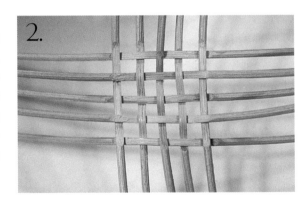

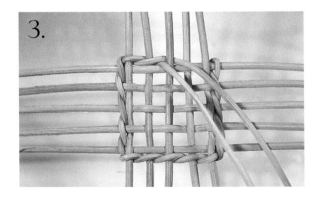

3. Take the most flexible weaver you have been soaking and bend it not quite in half, so that the ends will not need to be replaced at the same time. Now you are ready to begin twining. Place the bent reed around the left-most spoke on one side. Weave the top half of the weaver to the right, over the bottom half of the weaver, over the first spoke, then under the second. Do the same with the bottom weaver, alternating weavers after each over/under step.

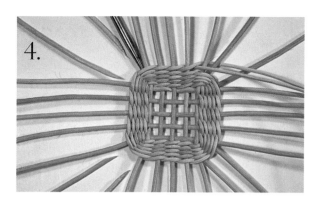

4. Continue all the way around four times. At the end of each row or two, use an awl to compact the weave. Notice there are large spaces at the corners and that more spokes need to be added. Measure the length of any original spoke from the edge of the grid to the end of the spoke and add one inch to insert into the weave. Cut eight pieces this length with long points at one end. Use an awl to open up the spaces to the insides of the two corner spokes. Insert two spokes per corner, one per space. Insert the remaining six spokes.

5. To begin the tapestry, which will keep the base square, find a very flexible, soaked, dark grey weaver. Cut a sharp point on one end and insert it into the space just to the right of the first inserted spoke or between the two new spokes in the same general space as the first new spoke. Weave to the right over and around the second added spoke. Go back to the left, over and around the first added spoke. Moving to the right, go over the second added spoke, then under and around the next spoke, which is an original spoke. Moving to the left, go under the second added spoke, over the first added spoke, then under and around the next spoke, which is an original spoke. Moving to the right, go under the first added spoke, over and around the second added spoke, then back to the left over and around the first added spoke. End the weaver in the same space as the second added spoke.

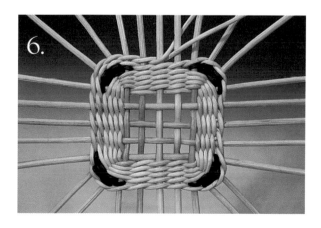

6. Weave the remaining three corners, repeating the same tapestry technique. Weave or twine four full rows, around the tapestry corners. Compact the weave all the way around the grid, encouraging it to define a square shape.

7. When you begin the fifth row, replace one, then a second natural weaver with dark grey weavers and add two more dark grey weavers. See Round Grid Tray with "Hairy" Sides, Photo and Instruction 5 on page 55.

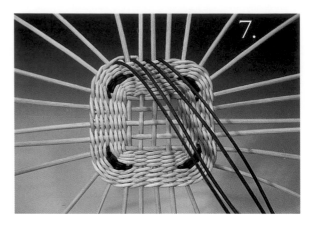

8. Weave one row with a 4-rod wale, then add a fifth dark grey weaver. The transition from two natural weavers to four dark grey weavers and then five dark grey weavers will give the base more interest and dimension.

9. Weave two rows with a 5-rod wale and stop. To bring the base back into a strong square, do a second set of tapestry weaves at each corner. Now you will need a very flexible natural weaver. Begin in the space of the first added spoke. Moving to the right, go over the second added spoke, then under and around the next spoke, which is an original. Moving to the left, go under the second added spoke, over the first added spoke, then under and around the next spoke, which is an original. Moving to the right, go under the first added spoke, over and around the second added spoke, then over and around the first added spoke. End the weaver in the general space between the first and second added spokes, then into the space of the second added spoke. Repeat the tapestry in natural reed, on the other three corners. Continue weaving for four rows with a 5-rod wale.

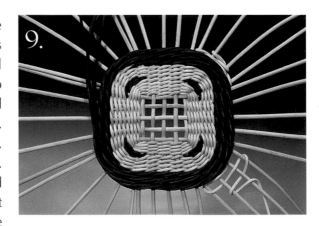

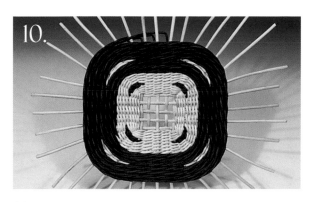

10. Just past the end of the fourth row, end each weaver over three and under two. See Begin and End Weavers on pages 17–18.

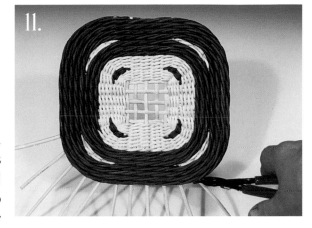

11. Tighten and encourage the weave to be as square as possible. Cut off the exposed spokes at the edge of the weave. This technique, using short spokes for the base, is especially useful when beginning a large basket, because you do not have to handle very long spokes. Also, should a spoke accidentally break anywhere in the basket, you can replace the broken spoke by inserting a new pointed spoke in along side the broken spoke. Just be certain that the two spokes overlap so as not to weaken that part of the basket.

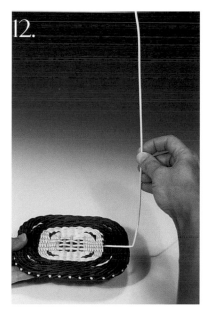

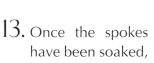

12. Measure new spokes by figuring 2" to go into the weave, plus the height of the basket (shown here about 5") plus 9"–10" for the rim. Measure and cut one new spoke for each one you cut off in Instruction 11. There are 36 spokes. Soak the spokes.

13. Once the spokes have been soaked, insert them all the way around, crimp each one just as it emerges from the base, then gently bend them upward.

14. Gently and loosely hold all the ends together to visualize the shape you are going to weave. Weave with a 4-rod wale with four natural weavers. When the basket measures 2" in height, replace one of the natural weavers with a dark grey weaver. Weave five rows, then replace the dark grey weaver with a natural weaver, skip one weaver, then replace the next natural weaver with a grey weaver. Weave three rows, then replace the other natural weavers with four dark grey weavers. Continue weaving with a 4-rod wale until the basket measures 5" in height. Loosely loop two spokes behind two spokes, then out. Continue all the way around, threading the last two through the first group. Turn the basket upside down and place it into warm/hot water for a few minutes to soak.

FINISHING THE INSIDE-OUT RIM

15. **Step 1** — Undo the loosely looped spokes, then tighten the weave all the way around and even up any unevenness in the height or along the top edge before beginning to weave the rim. Moving to the right, take one spoke over one spoke, leaving it pointing to the inside. Continue all the way around. All spokes should be pointing in. You may need to loosen the first and second spokes in order to see where to thread in the last end.

16. **Step 2** — Moving to the right, take one spoke over two spokes and thread the end just over and beyond, but in the same general space where the second spoke comes through the rim. Continue all the way around.

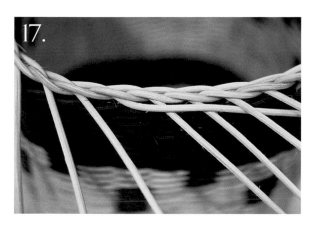

17. **Step 3** — With all the spokes pointing out away from the rim, take one spoke over two spokes, under one, then leave it. Continue all the way around.

18. This photo shows what Instruction 17 looks like midway around the rim. When you get around to the beginning, you may need to loosen the first two spokes.

19. To make the rim look heavier and more rounded, repeat Instruction 17.

20. It may be necessary to open up the first two spokes to see where to thread through the last two ends. See Finish on pages 20–21 for final shaping and singeing off any fuzz.

ROUND GRID TRAY
WITH "HAIRY" SIDES

Finished size: 2½" height x 12" width

This basket uses approximately 3 oz. of natural and 4 oz. of dark grey #3 reed for weavers and 2 oz. of natural #4 reed for spokes.

1. Follow Square Grid Instructions 1–4 on pages 48–49. In this basket, the spokes are 35" long. As you begin the sixth row, twine across it, stopping short of the first new spoke you added. This photo shows three completed sides and the work beginning on the first step of the last side. Notice how the ends of both weavers are pointing away, going between two different sets of spokes.

2. With the weavers going through the same sets of spokes at the end of the first side, turn the base over. The weavers will now be on the left. Notice the carved backs of the spokes in the center of the grid. This becomes the outside bottom of the basket. Working to the right and beginning with the left-most weaver, twine across this side. Weave over the first spoke and the other weaver, then under the next spoke. Repeat with the other weaver. Continue, alternating weavers, then stop short of the new spoke, leaving the weavers pointing away, as you did on the front side in Instruction 1.

54

3. Turn the base over again. The rounded sides of the grid's spokes should be facing you in the center of the grid. The weavers will again be on the left.

Note: The tapestry will fill in the areas necessary to make the grid square into a circle.

4. Twine across the tapestry you have just done. As you begin the second side, leave the second new spoke paired up with its spoke. You will "open it up" when you lay in the tapestry. In this photo, the tapestry is finished and just beginning to twine two rows, using new and old spokes evenly, thus encouraging the base to become round.

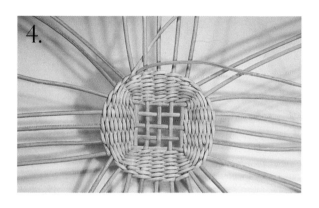

5. As you begin the third row since doing the tapestry, add two more weavers. The trick here is to make the transition as invisible as possible. Add one weaver on the left side of the general space where the second weaver comes forward, but have the new weaver go immediately behind the next spoke, then come forward. Do the same with the second new weaver. You now have four weavers and can weave over two spokes, under two with a 4-rod wale.

6. Continue weaving for two rows. At the same corner where you added the two weavers, add one more. Notice where the next available space is for a weaver to come forward, i.e. the space between two spokes where the next 4-rod wale weaver would have come forward. Work backwards two spokes so that the new weaver looks as if it had just gone behind two spokes and it came forward. Weave once around, going over three spokes, under two, with a 5-rod wale.

7. To enhance the thickness you created with five weavers, go from five weavers to two weavers and twine for two rows. To ensure an even number of rows, end one of the five weavers at the point of reference by going over three spokes, under two, then end. Repeat this with the next two weavers. Two weavers will remain. With these, twine two full rows. The 5-rod wale will stand out.

8. After the two rows of twining, add two more weavers at the point of reference. Weave three rows with a four rod wale. To finish the base, end each of the four weavers at the point of reference. Weave over two spokes, under two, then end. Repeat with each weaver. Since the spokes are now more than an inch apart, you will need to add an extra spoke to every other spoke. Use an awl to make room for the new spokes. To determine the length of the new spokes, cut a point on the end of a long piece of #5 reed. Insert this at least 1" into the base, next to an existing spoke. Cut the new spoke off at a length to match the existing spokes. Pull out the new spoke and use it as a guide for cutting 13 additional spokes. Insert these, then soak the base.

9. Cut and soak a handful of 5"-long pieces of dark grey reed. Tighten the base and even up any area which does not look round. Crimp new and old spokes. Insert five weavers, then weave once all the way around, opening up the new spokes. Make certain the weave is tight up against the base. (If you prefer, you can use four weavers.) Hold the spokes at a 90° angle as you weave. The side you have been working on will be showing on the inside of the basket with the spokes coming up around it.

10. As you begin to weave the second row, stop to insert one "hairy" piece behind each of the next few spokes, weave again over the "hairy" pieces and alternate weaving and inserting. During this second row of weaving, you will continue to hold the spokes at a 90° angle and pull hard enough to make them stand up. As you continue working, keep a gentle pressure on the weavers in order to keep the tension.

Note: Too much tension will cause the sides to close in, too little and the sides will flare out.

11. A view from above to show the "hairy" pieces being placed behind each spoke. After the spokes stand up by themselves, relax the tension on the weavers and maintain the shape with weaving, which is neither loose nor tight. At this point, you will be able to add a full row of "hairy" pieces behind each spoke, then follow it with a row of weaving. It is very important to tighten the weave every two or three rows since this is what holds the "hairy" pieces in place.

12. Finish off the weavers by weaving over three, then end for a 5-rod wale (or over two and end for 4-rod wale) all the way around. Soak the basket in order to weave off the rim. Once soaked, tighten the weave all the way around and add one more row of "hairy" pieces. Finish off the rim. See Finishing the Rim Instructions 16–21 on pages 35–36.

Note: Interesting variations to this basket would be to begin the grid with sets of double spokes, i.e. using five sets of two spokes in each direction or use dyed spokes for the grid.

The "Hairy" Technique

The idea for the "hairy" technique came during a visit to England. My cousin and his wife had constructed an informal aviary. They gave their birds little commercially made baskets to "nest" in. These were smooth, shallow, colorless, and had to be wired to a branch. I told them I would try to make something better. I went home and came up with a "nest". The inside was the size of half an orange. I wove dozens of 4" rattan twigs, in shades of beige, and brown, and muted orange, and pink into the structure of the basket. As soon as I finished the "nest", I knew I had started something important. Finally, here was a way to work with lots of color changes without worrying about how to hide and secure all the ends. For lack of anything more technical, I sentimentally call this the "hairy" technique after my cousin, Harry.

I went on to use the "hairy" technique in larger baskets and to experiment with how and where to use its texture. Sometimes I wove the "hairy" pieces sticking out into the center/inside of a basket and watched how the outside developed an interesting pattern. Sometimes the "hairy" pieces were trapped between the inside and outside of a double-wall construction. Here, I had to leave the top surface unwoven so you could appreciate the texture inside. Spherical forms worked well to show off color progressions as they drew to a close at the rim.

Lately, I have been using the "hairy" pieces more to create subtle surfaces, rather than splurging with the excitement of colors, as shown in the double-wall piece "Building Momentum" on page 64. Seeing hundreds of pieces bundled together by color still tempts me to take them out and weave color studies.

ROUND & "HAIRY"
WITH WOVEN RIM

Finished size: 8" height x 9½" width

This basket uses approximately 4 oz. of dark grey, 4 oz. of red, and 1 oz. of natural #3 reed for weavers and "hairy" pieces and 2 oz. of dark grey #4 reed for spokes.

1. Cut several bundles of #3 reed, 5" long, for "hairy" pieces, and 14 spokes, 34" long, then soak them all in warm/hot water. Do not worry about exact numbers for the "hairy" pieces, since you can cut and soak more as you need them. The inside diameter of the wall will be approximately 6", so you need more than 10 spokes, but less than 20. Since a woven rim uses less length, you only have to add 6" at each spoke end. Choose strands which have strength, but also flexibility, in order to weave off the rim later.

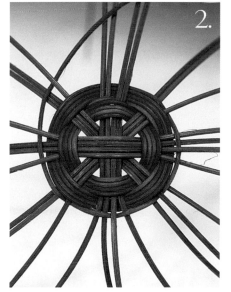

2. Since 14 spokes cannot be divided into four equal parts, first cross two groups of three spokes each, then place two groups of four spokes each on top of them. See Vertical Pattern with 4- & 6-rod Wale Instruction 1 on page 31. Bind over four spokes, then under three, four times. Make the transition, bind under four spokes, then over three, four times. As you are about to bind over three for a fifth time, use an awl to open up the spokes sideways, and weave over two spokes, behind one, then give the weaver a pull, over two, behind one, pull. Continue all the way around three times.

3. After three rows, check for the point of reference. See Point of Reference on pages 18–19, so you know where to start adding the "hairy" pieces. You may need to add a few pieces, weave a bit, add a few pieces, etc., alternating pieces and weaving until eventually you will be able to add a full row, weave a row, etc. See Round Grid Tray with "Hairy" Sides, Photos 10–12 on page 57. Once you have completed a full row of "hairy" pieces followed by a row of over/behind weaving, stop.

5. At the top of photo 5, notice where the new weavers were added and where the "hairy" pieces were added. The four weavers are shown having been woven ⅔ of the way around. When you finish two rows of "hairy" pieces and two rows of 4-rod wale, compact the weave. See Tighten & Compact for Strength on pages 15–16. This will keep the "hairy" pieces locked into the weave, repeat this after every two or three rows of weaving.

4. At this point, add three more weavers. Weaving with four weavers will make a sturdier basket. (Here, the inside of the basket is shown.) Add the first new weaver in the general space to the right of the existing weaver. Moving to the right, add two more weavers. Once the three additional weavers have been added, add a row of "hairy" pieces. Working to the right, begin weaving over two spokes, behind two, with a 4-rod wale.

6. Continue weaving and adding pieces alternately. To shape the basket, gently pull on the weavers as you weave. If the opening (circumference) comes in too quickly, you are pulling too hard. See Crimp & Shape on pages 16–17. Remember to tighten by holding onto two or more spokes and pulling. If when you do this, the shape flattens out, you need to increase the tension on the weavers as you go around. As you reach the half way point (at the basket's greatest diameter), the tension will be minimal. As you begin to close in the form, increase the tension again slightly.

7. You will know when to stop because you will not be able to weave anymore, and you need some room for the woven rim. Finish off the weavers over two spokes, then end. Continue all the way around. Soak the basket. Before beginning the rim, tighten the weave one last time, then add the last row of "hairy" pieces.

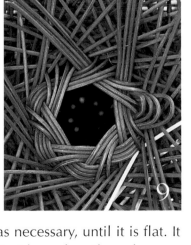

8. Since you have 28 spoke ends (2 x 14 spokes), you can evenly divide these by four into seven groups (if you were using 20 spokes, 40 spoke ends, you could weave this rim with groups of four or five spokes). Moving to the right, take four spokes behind four spokes, then leave them pointing out. Once each group has gone behind the next, adjust any spokes that are not lying flat.

9. Cut the spokes to 4" before trying to work them into the basket. Take them one at a time, pulling them gently to flatten them, over two spokes in the next group and thread in each one. Play with the rim, tightening or loosening as necessary, until it is flat. It is not necessary to trim off the excess spokes inside, unless they show or technically interfere with the rim lying flat.

DOUBLE-WALL CONSTRUCTION

The double-wall constructions are where my experience, experiments, training, and techniques all come together. They confront me with the opportunity to exercise and challenge my mind. They both lure me and force me to take risks and develop new ideas. Each construction is different. I enjoy the process of problem solving, but sometimes the answers do not come easily. When the ideas work, I feel brilliant, when they do not, I take the basket apart and try something different.

The idea of making a double-wall construction came from my background in pottery—I liked pots with heavy rims. To create this in a basket, I first came up with the "inner edge." To take this another step further I developed the double-wall construction. These "thick" edges gave the baskets an illusion of weight.

To add an element of surprise to the pieces, I added rocks or marbles, wood or seed pods just before joining the inner and outer baskets together. Sometimes the reason was as simple as wanting the extra weight. Other times there was a story involved. "Architexture," a green and natural "hairy" piece with exposed spokes, contains pieces of oak molding from a renovation project. This piece was woven in tribute and in memory to my mother, who left me the money with which to "build". In another basket, "Path to My Garden," a wide, shallow green form, a tapestry path leads you

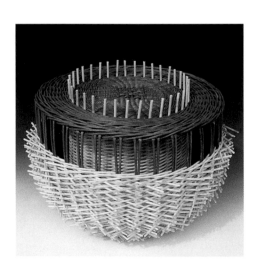

  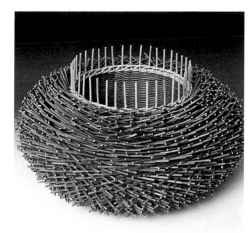

across a green field to a sunken garden. There is a chamber below the garden that holds two large seed pods. These hold the abstract promise of new life. This basket combines two of my greatest passions, art and gardening.

Double-wall constructions are about problem solving and using everything you know to come up with something uniquely your own. Here I show you what went into making three of these pieces to give you ideas about how you can build something from your own imagination. These pieces, like all the others in this book, are meant to be springboards for your own creativity.

  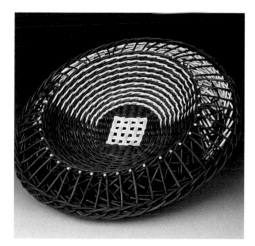

BUILDING MOMENTUM

Finished size: 6" height x 12" width

1. For the inner basket, I started with a five-spoke by five-spoke grid base. When the base measured 4½" in width, I stopped and crimped the spokes so they stood up, added a new spoke next to each existing spoke, then crimped each of these so they pointed down. With the spokes pointing down, I wove a hidden basket to support the inner basket.

2. A close-up showing the original spokes going up and the new added spokes pointing down.

3. The hidden lower basket is finished. The upper basket is woven with the "hairy" technique showing on the inside.

4. The outer basket is woven using a reverse tapestry pattern. I did this by altering the tapestry technique. See Becoming Band with Double Tapestry Stripes Instruction 2 on page 42. Here I added each new tapestry piece in the general space one back from the previous row.

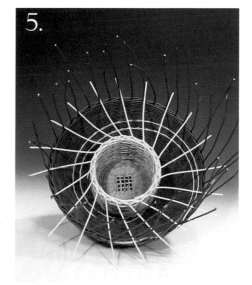

5. I wove the rim on the inner basket inside out, leaving the spokes pointing out, then I crimped the spokes. I placed the baskets one inside the other to check for height. At this point, it was easier to adjust the height by undoing the hidden basket's rim and adding or subtracting rows as necessary.

6. As I worked on the top, I added more spokes so that there were the same number of spokes coming out of the top as there were coming up in the outer basket. After a final check for fit, I cut the spokes of the inner basket flush to the edge of the weave.

7. The inner basket was lowered into the outer basket and the outer basket's rim joined the two together. See Blue/Purple Oval Instructions 4–5 on page 67.

PLAYING FIELD

Finished size: 10" height x 19½" width

1. This basket began as three separate pieces. First, I wove the outer basket, then started the grid top, then wove the inner basket up to support the grid top at the same level as the top of the outer basket. The top was woven out to where the inner spokes came up, then the weaving continued beyond the exposed spokes until it reached the outer edge. I crimped the top's spokes, then inserted them into the outer basket's walls, to hold all three baskets together.

Note: Just before the top's weaving reached and enclosed the inner basket's spokes, I placed round objects inside to be "played with" in another reality.

BLUE/PURPLE OVAL

Finished size: 14¾" height x 18½" width x 12" depth

1. I wove the stepped tapestry pattern, using a variation on the tapestry technique. The stripes were woven by replacing all five blue weavers with five natural weavers, weaving half-way around the basket, then replacing the natural weavers with blue weavers again. I wove a full row of blue in between the half-natural/half-blue rows to maintain wall strength. To create the oval, I pressed in on the sides, then wove in partial rows at each end. Without the extra rows at each end, the pushed-in sides would be higher than the ends. The partial rows were added and staggered as necessary to maintain the height of the walls at each end.

2. This photo shows the finished inner basket. The spokes were cut off flush with the outer edge. I wove the hidden basket after the upper part of the inner basket was completed.

Note: The oval inner basket needed partial rows to build up their ends as was done in the outer basket.

3. The height of the inner basket was checked and if adjustments were needed, the height of the outer basket was altered. These changes could have also been made to the height of the hidden basket.

4. To finish the rim, moving to the right, I took one spoke behind one spoke, then brought it forward and continued all the way around the rim. I threaded the last spoke through the first spoke or rim, so it, too, stuck out. Sometimes I find it is easier to do this step before I put one basket inside the other.

5. I gently pulled a spoke, counted over four spokes, then inserted it through the rim of the outer basket into the top of the inner basket, into a space shared by a cut off spoke, then I added marbles before the two baskets were completely joined.

Note: Notice how the stripes seem to flare at the ends on this inside view of the finished basket. This is where partial rows were added to build up the ends.

INVITED ARTISTS

As a new century begins, technology is king and handwork is suspect. Why do long-division if you have a calculator? Why write a letter long-hand if you can do it on a computer? Time is at a premium. Personal expression is harder to find.

Contemporary basket makers are challenging technology and mass produciton by creating works of art, using new techniques and available materials. They can choose nearly any material they want and then discover a way to use them. The time spent making them can be physically challenging or meditative, depending on the artists' needs. Inspiration can take the form of a highrise or a bend in a branch. What unites these basket makers is that each of them has become a master of their particular medium or process.

They have taken their work beyond the safe and expected and ventured into the unknown. When it works, it becomes "art", when it does not, they go back to work and try again. They have defined themselves as basket makers, sculptors, and artists. I invite you to see how they work, what they have to say, and marvel at their ingenuity and creativity.

Photo by Bromhead Photography
Detail: "White Willow Grid Bowl"
by Dail Behennah

Photo by Russell Johnson
Detail: "My Father Turning into a
Luscombe"
by John McQueen

Photo by Jeff Baird
Detail: "Double Basket"
by JoAnne Russo

68

DOROTHY GILL BARNES

I delight in the outdoors and the variety of fiber materials I discover there. Being careful to only use wood that is slated to be thinned or cleared, I weave, scar, and carve the natural materials into nontraditional baskets and sculptures.

Beginning in the '50s as an instructor of art education, I provided materials for my classes and studio from conventional sources, purchasing pigments, paper, and clay. Nearly thirty years ago, I started making baskets with an interest in contemporary forms, collecting materials found in nature. My first basket was coiled from iris leaves wilting in our backyard. I used a sharp bone as an awl, reminiscent of how it might have been made more than 7,000 years ago. This transition to using materials discovered in nature has become the essential part of my work. I want especially to harvest responsibly, using the precious, beautiful bark, roots, and wood with respect for the landscape. As I travel when teaching, I find amazing variety in vegetation and often have the delightful opportunity to harvest in faraway places. I am fortunate also to have requests to cut in an Ohio basket willow copse, to thin young pine at a tree farm, and permission to take bark from freshly felled trees at a sawmill nearby. Here in my suburban yard I sometimes graft, wrap, or mark growing weed trees for use later.

Photo by Doug Martin
Arrowmont Poplar—1998
20" x 22" x 11"

I appreciate the special opportunity I have to use these precious trees and to learn about their bark. This outer skin between the wood and the elements has such glorious properties. I am amazed at the variety of texture and color, strength and delicacy—cork, hickory, cedar, madrone, sycamore, pine—both old and young. This supply of art materials is inexhaustible, inspiring in its diversity, and takes me to wondrous places to find it.

When I make a basket, it is an object with an interior space related to carrying or holding something. I enjoy the connection with traditional basketry. I am amazed at the complex weaves and problem solving to build containers needed over the centuries.

I enjoy seeing chaos in material and putting order into it. I like for the process to show. I do not usually care for fly-away, distracting embellishments.

The materials are the reason I make baskets. It is a joy to harvest in nature, identifying the proper trees to cut and using them in an innovative way. I only rarely use wire, bolts, staples, cords, etc., as needed in problem solving, but the primary material is found in nature or grown by me. I choose the material for its strength, color, flexibility, and availability. It is seasonal, very time-consuming, and often hard, dirty work to prepare, but I love it!

The making-time varies. My work can be done in minutes or take years. Recently, I pulled an 18'-long strip of heavy bark from a basswood tree. There in the woods, I scored and folded it into a finished piece. The inside dimensions of my van dictated the size and form of it. This took a couple of hours.

Some pieces take many years because the design is growing on a designated live tree (one that must be cut within a few years). I call these designs "dendroglyphs." At home, as I prepare branch bark, limbs, roots, etc., I lay out my harvest and study it. Partly made

Photo by Doug Martin

Pleated Bark Box—1997
4½" x 8" x 6"

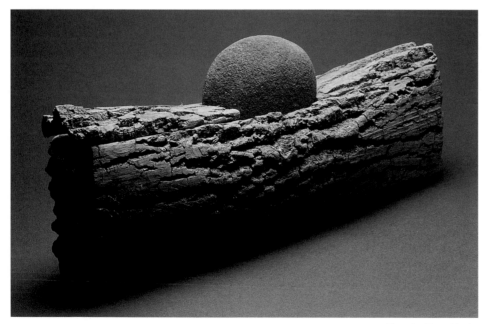

pieces are all over the place. Some ready to assemble, some waiting for spring to get the extra material I need to finish.

I sometimes draw a reminder sketch when I have so many pieces in progress or in my head, but mostly work directly with the material.

Chance is very important in my work. Chance to hear a chain saw at the right time. Chance to find yard trash—and in construction experimentation, often strange unexpected shrinkage will hold a stone just right. Some things cannot be planned.

Photo by Doug Martin

Stone Bark Box—1997
6" x 16" x 4"

DAIL BEHENNAH

I studied geography at university and was particularly interested in drawing maps. This interest in grids, fine lines, symbols, and information has remained with me.

When I left university, I had several office jobs, but I knew that I wanted to do something else. All the women in my family make things and it is our principal form of relaxation. I have knitted, stitched, and embroidered since childhood and after I left university, I tried many crafts at evening classes before discovering basketry. This literally added another dimension, enabling fine lines and grids to be drawn in the air.

I have deliberately avoided things that I do not like, notably wet materials and weaving. In order to avoid these, I have had to find new solutions to problems in constructing vessels and this in turn has meant that my baskets are easily identifiable as my work, and gives them a unity. The border used on the pebble dishes is one I developed myself, although I would not be surprised to find it on baskets that have been made for centuries—I just do not know about them.

To create the central grid, groups of three pieces of Poeluti cane are plaited in an over-one, under-one pattern, then tied onto the mould.

Two long pieces of cane are placed on either side of the grid and tightly twined onto it, following the edge of the mould. On the second row, the two rows are also coiled together, using blue or green wire. This strengthens the structure and creates the stitching pattern. On the final row of the border, the ends of the grid canes are cut off and the long border canes are tapered before being finished with a double stitch.

Pebbles and shells are drilled, threaded onto telephone wire, and lashed onto the basket, creating diagonal lines across the grid.

My latest pieces are stacks of willow grids, carved into in various ways to make bowls. These are carefully worked out on graph paper and then pieces of willow are cut to length, drilled and threaded together. The stack of grids changes from two to three dimensions as the viewer moves around the basket. The shadows cast by these baskets are as significant as the containers themselves.

I like working on a series of pieces. As I work with the material, lots of ideas come to me, but because the process takes so long, I cannot afford to risk ruining what I have already done by trying out something new, so I do it in the next piece, by which time I have had time to think through the idea properly.

Brown Willow Grid Bowl with Peeled Hollow—1998
5" x 16" x 16"

Dish with Pebbles & Shells—1992
4½" x 21" x 21"

I sketch vague diagrams of an idea with masses of annotations around them, usually on scraps of paper or the backs of envelopes. Sometimes I find these months later and find that I have incorporated the idea into a basket without realizing it. The act of putting it onto paper seems to fix it in my mind and the drawing is no longer necessary. Occasionally I collect up the pieces of paper and copy the ideas all together onto one sheet.

I think the very Englishness of the colors evokes wet and windswept beaches and that is why people like my baskets. They trigger memories and this way, my memories of happiness get passed around to other people.

I am also working on a series of organic forms made from Poeluti cane stitched with silver colored wire. They resemble leaves, seed pods, and vessels. I like the slow rhythmic stitching on these coiled pieces.

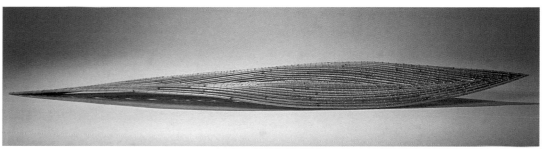

Long Coiled Dish
2½" x 39" x 7"

White Willow Grid Bowl
7" x 17¾" x 17¾"

It is good to make coiled and grid baskets together as the spontaneity and rhythm of the coiling is a good antidote to the concentration and precision of the grids.

When I was at school, I used to draw sheets of knotted and tangled rope. It is how I feel inside, but my work appears very clam, restrained, and polite; and I think that is how people regard me, too. My baskets are an attempt to bring order and form to the knotted and tangled rope.

Many things influence me. I am always looking at things, and naturally pay particular attention to baskets from around the world and other contemporary crafts. I am especially interested in jewelry and textiles. However, I am rarely conscious of any specific influence when I am making a piece; but later I may look at it and realize that it was inspired by something I have seen.

JAN BUCKMAN

Work In Progress

"My work comes from the contrast between what is, and what was; what was, and what can be." This is from an artist statement I wrote over 15 years ago.

Change, leaving what was and moving toward what can be, can be frustrating, even frightening, as well as exhilarating and rewarding. With my earlier baskets, I had chosen to work within the boundaries of symmetry and familiar shapes utilizing my long-time ally, graph paper. At the time, bark had become a compelling and welcome substance in my hands, but a foreigner in the realm of my baskets. My first mistake was attempting to make the bark conform to the

Detail: 1.0 mm drilled holes

Detail: Wrapped Twining Technique

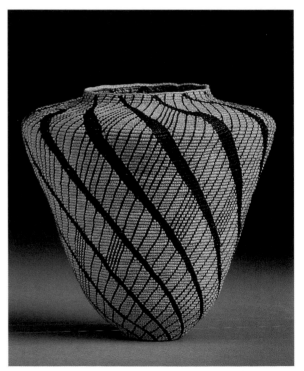

Untitled #8-2
Twined in Waxed Linen—1992
5¾" x 6"

rigid confines I had set for these baskets. It did not work.

Although I still process the bark by peeling, drying, and finishing, I now try to impose on it as little as possible. The waxed linen is attached to, but not dependent on the bark—relating to, but not attempting to define the bark. My task is to get these disparate media to talk to each other, row by row, word by word, sentence by sentence. It is a conversation that continues between the bark—my unruly friend, and the linen—my dependable comrade, throughout the entire journey.

A word on process: the linen is

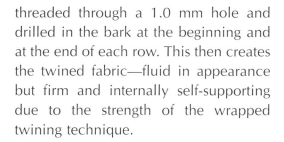
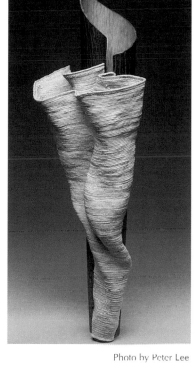

threaded through a 1.0 mm hole and drilled in the bark at the beginning and at the end of each row. This then creates the twined fabric—fluid in appearance but firm and internally self-supporting due to the strength of the wrapped twining technique.

What am I doing? As before, creating things which I find (and I trust others do) appealing on a number of levels. What do they mean? Whatever you like. For me a change… trying to better articulate the dialogue between the man-made and what is natural, between my need to create and my ability to appreciate what is already there. What is… and what can be…

Above: Conversion III—1999
17" x 5" x 6"

Left: Untitled #8-4
Twined in Waxed Linen—1994
6" x 4"

Right: Untitled #12-10
Twined in Waxed Linen—1990
6" x 4⅝"

Cutting lace.

KEN CARLSON

My background is in traditional leatherwork. In the process of teaching myself the countless variations of braids, I began to explore plaiting as an art—experimenting with nontraditional applications of classic braiding techniques. This led me to conceive of leather baskets. Working from a foundation of traditional plaiting techniques, I developed methods to give structure and form to leather's flexible nature.

My initial exploration into basketry in leather led to experimenting with copper, another nontraditional material. Copper has unique qualities. It is ductile yet structural, pliable yet rigid. Its nature allows the creation of unusual, architectural shapes. It took a while to develop techniques to best exploit copper's nature, and my first experiments were influenced by works in other media. Kari Lønning's double-walled baskets intrigued me and tempted me to experiment with the various forms double-walled copper pieces could take. Architectural designs, both modern and ancient, also contributed. Some of the

Joining two panels with a simulated 8-strand round braid.

Weaving a 16-strand flat braid.

pieces departed from being vessels and entered the realm of sculpture. Some were clearly influenced by the graphic works of M. C. Escher.

When I work, I cut thin copper strips and then weave these together into three dimensional shapes. Once the forms are completed, I use copper's tendency to react with chemicals to form patinas, to give the surface both texture and color. Unfortunately, the toxic nature of some of the chemicals has recently forced me to abandon copper due to health concerns and to return to working primarily in leather.

Porcupine Basket—1989
9" x 9"
woven and patinaed copper

My approach has always been to push the envelope of form and technique with any material I use. Having no background in basketry and being completely self-taught has engendered an attitude of experimentation and freedom. Making baskets from nontraditional materials presents interesting challenges and in my opinion, is one hell of a lot of fun. I enjoy the whole process and I like the fact that the results then challenge the viewer to see basketry, as well as copper and leather, in a new light.

Left: Waterfall—1993
10¾" x 7" x 7"
woven and patinaed copper

Right: Tall Spiral—1995
27" x 5"
woven and patinaed copper

Basket Form—1998
5" x 5"
geometric flat braid and round braid edge

Tulip—1986
8" x 10"
22-strand flat braid, 10-strand flat braid, and
simulated 8-strand round braid

Cylinder Form—1985
11½" x 5"
10-strand flat braid and simulated 8-strand round braid edge

Photo by David Kingsbury

Evidence—1997
20" x 18" x 18"
tire bits, bullet-riddled steel, copper and steel wires, fabric,
and beads

I have been intrigued with using ordinary, cast-off, found, and salvaged materials in my art for a very long time. No doubt this interest was engendered by my father who set me to the task of straightening nails in his workshop when I was a child. Since I live in a culture of excess and planned obsolescence, I have a myriad of materials with which to work. I am challenged by these materials and my imagination to build inventive structures that give these materials a new life.

In making my basket forms, I often construct a flat mat first. The materials might be woven on themselves or interlaced through hardware cloth, a manufactured wire grid. This flat construction is then folded into a three dimensional form. Some forms are made from salvaged pieces of sheet copper. The oxidized surfaces remind me of the New Mexican landscape, adobe houses, and rustling tin roofs, as well as topographical details viewed from an airplane. These forms are held in place with rivets. Other times, I build armatures from plied wire into which I interlace various materials.

Baskets have many associations with human activities. Most are related to domestic life, especially to food preparation and storage. But baskets have been used for other functions including games, decoration, the exhibition of status, and the display of human skill and ingenuity. Inspired by these many associations and my abundant materials, I strive to create my own provocative visual poems.

Left: Tract—1993
13" x 18" x 18"
copper, wire, and rivets

Right: Pod Basket for
the Solstice Sun—
1992
16" x 20"
painted aluminum,
hardware cloth, wire,
beads, and sequins

Birch plywood is painted, varnished, and cut to size.

My work is informed by an interest in architectural space, and in music, its structure and rhythm. Manipulations of space are a central theme. I originally trained in textiles, constructing and manipulating surfaces and making objects. The three dimensional nature of this work, the relationship between surface, structure, and space led to the study of basketry. This early training has underlain and formed much of my work since.

Much of my time is divided between my studio and time spent traveling, teaching, or working as a visiting artist. The periods away from the studio allow space to draw, write, think, develop ideas, and do background reading. Studio time is one of intense making, often on a group of works that explore a common set of ideas. The working process involves a dialogue between the material substance of the object and the idea.

The first layer of weaving is formed. This layer controls the final curve of the dish.

Over the years, I have used a diverse range of materials and techniques, from weaving to welding, from thread to steel. The choice of material and technique is connected with the underlying intention at least as much as with practical structural necessity.

The grid—woven, stitched, painted, or implied—acts as a unifying and underlying structure mapping the surface. The curved planes create forms which define and interact with space occupied and space contained, of sound and silence.

Further layers are added, and held in place temporarily with clothespins.

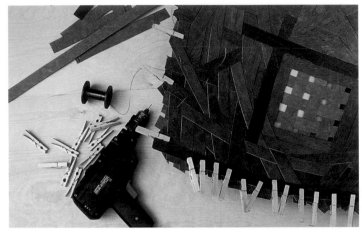

Holes are drilled for the stitching that holds the edges together. Finally, the edges will be trimmed.

The swell of the curved dishes lifts them up from their ground and reveals the dark underside, creating an interplay between surfaces. The rhythm of the layers of woven surfaces lead the eye into the structure, into its depths. There is movement between the layers, and an interplay of order and disorder.

Blue Line—1996
6" x 21" x 23"
interlaced, painted, and dyed birch plywood and wire stitching

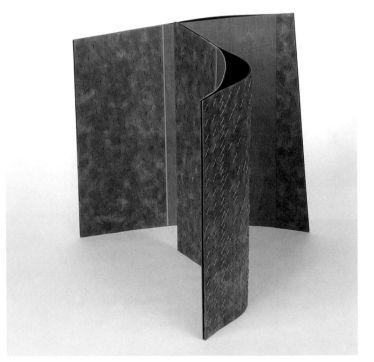

Something About the Way the Light Falls—1996
18" x 20" x 4" each
laminated and painted birch plywood and wire stitching

In other works, the smooth plywood surface is intended to lead the eye over and around the taut curves. The layers of interacting surfaces and spaces in these works imply a much larger, architectural sense of space and structure. The walls and the curves of empty space contain structural tensions. The pairings interact but do not touch. Perhaps the plywood surfaces also hint at a distant memory of bark vessels.

Marks of construction write messages through the forms. The stitching holds the work together, but has two faces, it travels through the structure from front to back—front implies back, implies space and meaning between.

Section of a larger installation: Shadows Cross
the Square—1996
6" x 21" x 21"
interlaced, painted, and dyed birch plywood, willow bark,
and wire stitching

Between Walls—1996
20" x 22" x 4" each
laminated birch plywood and wire stitching

Having recently returned from an extended visit to Australia, I have found myself thinking about the desert, an "empty" space. In consequence, my recent work explores the question of whether a work can be both a flat expanding field—an "empty" space—and an object; there is an attempt to reconcile this paradox.

The increasingly understated, pared down nature of recent works places demands upon the viewer. Complex, layered ideas are distilled to their essences, leaving trace-memories, hints, and implications. A large part of the working process involves a taking away of what is inessential. There is increasingly a search for stillness—for the space between.

FERNE JACOBS

Making the work feels feminine, slow rhythms spiraling, centered in a state of being rather than thrusting outward; creating with a sense of the timeless; feeling outside of technology; listening to something within.

This is a form of classicism; trying to stay with a form until it is done and feels complete. The excitement for me is in the details, going so slow that I spend a great amount of time in them. It is as if I find the form through the details, creating a body that emerges by each wrap of the thread, cell by cell.

Photo by Susan Einstein

Left: Figure—
1992–1993
27½" x 11" x 11"
coiled and twined
waxed linen
thread

Upper Right:
Unfolding Water—
1997–1998
43" x 37½" x 5"
coiled and twined
waxed linen
thread

Lower Right:
Landed Moon—
1997
12½" x 11" x 6½"
coiled and twined
waxed linen
thread

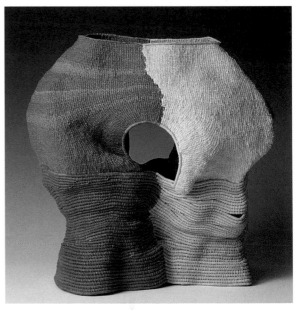

Photo by Susan Einstein

Photo by Susan Einstein

CHRISTINE E. JOY

The cycles of the seasons, always changing and repeating, the ordered movement of a year, plotted out in months and days, the weekly routine, the daily rhythm, the inevitable flow of time from birth to death, mysterious, astonishing, exciting, holding promise and life. This concept of time flowing in cycles, in circular motion, is a powerful influence on my basketry.

Willow grows in abundance in Montana. The building of my baskets begins with the harvesting of native twigs, which unites me with the cycles of the seasons. It expands my awareness of the richness of the earth and my dependency on it. There is a partnership between myself and the willow. I loosely conceive a form for the basket and as the form grows, I watch the patterns and movement that develop, changing my original idea as needed. The growth of a basket is always a surprise and I enjoy not knowing how the form will end. From the fruition of the basket's construction to the next harvest, I am involved in a representational cycle. The baskets become concrete symbols of the passage of my life.

The colors of the willow and red dogwood stand out so brightly in the winter months. It was the beauty of the branches that initially compelled me to try and make a basket. I wanted to put the sticks together in my own way, not following traditional weaving techniques. At first, bird nests were my inspiration and I used a collage of materials. It took several years of experimenting before my technique evolved to the point where I had a vessel form that was structurally sound. As I gained more control over the shaping, I found inspiration from a wide array of nature's vessels. It is the forms and movement in nature that continue to influence my work.

I construct my baskets to appear as if they are moving, growing, and animated, as though the shapes had been cut from a tree or pulled from moving water. I want my baskets to sit still,

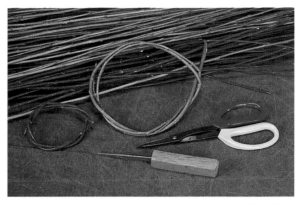

Photo by Tom Ferris

Tools and willow—all baskets begin with one stick formed into a circle.

Photo by Tom Ferris

"Bloom" at 4" x 11"

Photo by Tom Ferris

"Bloom" at 10" x 15"

Bloom—1999
12" x 17"
willow and red dogwood

Lamp—1995
8½" x 12" x 9"
willow and red dogwood

unchanging, yet to the eye of the viewer to flow, to move around and back again, to carry the movement of life within its form.

The purpose of my baskets is not so much to contain or carry goods, but is to carry a part of myself within its movement and shape.

Left: Listen—1994
19" x 19" x 14"
willow

Right: Crescent Moon—1996
27" x 30" x 13"
willow and red dogwood

MARKKU KOSONEN

Finland is known as a land of lakes and forest. But only three species of timber are industrially utilized. As an artist and craftsman, I want to bring forth the entire variety of the available tree species. I am, however, a patriot and will keep to the trees growing in Finland, of which there are some basic species. I want to develop tradition and heritage, not preserve it. Therefore my approach to the material and objects made from it is often the opposite of what is customary in industry or culture. I discovered willow as an aid when teaching crafts teachers the unity of design and making in crafts. Though wood, willow can be woven or plaited. In the course, a master basket maker showed how a real willow basket is made, and all the teachers obediently followed suit.

I was intimidated by the formal approach to learning and as a kind of protest, I made a "basket" in a way that was the complete opposite of the master's instructions. My "basket" interested the Museum of Art and Design in Helsinki, and it was only then that I realized that I had made something new. Until then, I had only worked with solid wood, with skill as my guiding concept.

I differ from the free artist only in that I am committed to a certain material. For me, the material has the role of a teacher and is not just a medium of self-expression. In most cases, I make my works directly from their final material. During the work, my thoughts have already passed to the next opportunity. Influences come from

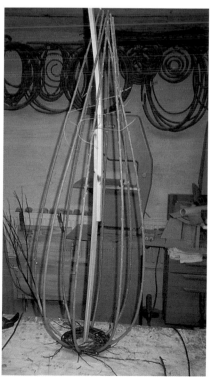

Willow and Growberry group shot

I often start to make a basket by relying on old tradition, but before long, I start to raise the rim towards strange themes. What begins as an ordinary utilitarian object soon turns into a creative work. Unstripped willow has opportunities for a grand new transformation, where it was previously used only in modest utility objects. Leaving the catkins in place, which is one of my trademarks, prompts most of the questions concerning my work. How do they stay on? Have they done something to them? It is incredible that no one believes they have naturally dried into place.

ideas, ideals, and the practical aspects of material and techniques. Design also requires the aspect of making an object in material terms, thus differing from drawn design.

My formal training consists of a carpentry and cabinet making school, followed by a design school. I have worked as a carpenter, interior architect, teacher, civil servant, critic, and journalist. Craftsmanship and wood have been the constant of all my work.

The Willow

Growing by the shoreline and along the edges of fields and barely utilized, the willow is readily regarded as one of our most useless wood species, if even accorded the status of wood. Its tenacity is seen in its ability to carve itself a place in the landscape shaped by man. It easily adapts from the countryside to urban conditions. It has been introduced into the towns and cities along railway lines, roads, and power lines. Growing between the foundations of houses and the surrounding asphalt, it forces itself into the best commercial locations. It is the first to grow in a vacant lot. The strong and irresistible message of adaptation and the miracle of growth bring man and willow closer together.

Birch Bark Dish—1998
4" x 11¾" x 19¾"

The heritage of willow objects is a continuum in which I represent the contemporary aspect. It is no longer significant to make traditional utility objects of willow to the same extent as in the past. New opportunities and uses must be found for willow. A new function is to be found in the symbols of the object, the tales and messages which the maker leaves of his personality. This is known as expression.

Translated by Juri Kokkonen

Left: Willow
Series—1997
group shot

Upper Right:
Birchbark Bowls—
1998
each is approximately 8" x 11¾"

Lower Right:
Willow I—1996
23½" x 27½"

GYÖNGY LAKY

I reach into adjacent fields to form my vessels. Fingers are my tools when I am basket making, but I have now found a 20th century tool that led me to new types of constructions. Using influences from furniture making, I work with an electric drill and use dowels—both traditional and nontraditional—to form my sculptural containers. My nontraditional doweling employs unusual items such as toothpicks, food skewers, nails, bolts, and screws. But it is the traditional, quintessential bowl—the vessel, the pure and concentrated form of an ingenious container—the basket—that inspires and informs my work in basketry.

The ability to reach out and gather some substance nearby and to transform it, to make something of it, is the brilliance of human ingenuity and inventiveness that attracts me to basket making. I use this age-old approach today. Sometimes my materials come from what I call the "industrial harvest"—that which society

Photo by Tom Grotta

Affirmative #1—1996
each piece 7¼" x 7¼" x 7¼"
plied and sewn telephone wire

casts off after fabrication and use—but, more often now, I employ tree trimmings. The cuttings come primarily from agricultural sources. In addition to the materials from fruit and nut trees, and some fruit vines, twigs from park and street tree pruning are used as well. Use of discarded materials or by-products has been a recurring theme in my work for more than 20 years and continues today. My earlier work incorporated mainly materials from commercial sources, such as plastic packaging, discarded telephone wire, or scrap cloth. My current work uses plum, apple, walnut, apricot, peach, cherry, almond, olive, and citrus cuttings, and from street trees, garden, and park sources, such as acacia, sycamore, and eucalyptus. By using the trimmings, growers and gardeners produce and discard in vast quantities each year, I am working with a specialized and excellent textile material formerly considered refuse. I am turning discards into art and helping to address the need to

Photo by Lee Fatheree

Thicket—1997
13" x 25"
apricot prunings doweled

reduce airborne particulate matter resulting from incineration of trimmings, which is still the preferred method of disposal for most growers in my area.

Antecedents which have extensively influenced my approach to textile form and structure in basketry came into my work from an early interest in what I refer to as "traditional textile architecture." This is the sculptural spectrum of textile objects and techniques of fabrication such as appear in the granaries of Mexico, baskets of India, reed boats of Bolivia, rope suspension bridges of the Andes, bamboo scaffolding of China, indigenous stick housing of American Indians, reed buildings of Iraq, thatched roofs of England and even as found in the woven branches used in gun emplacements at Quebec's Chateau Frontenac or used in land reclamation and erosion projects in the Netherlands. Fascination with these seminal and simple, textile inventions has led me to experiment with structures and materials emphasizing the possibilities inherent in dimensional linear arrangements employing simple procedures, humble materials, and the

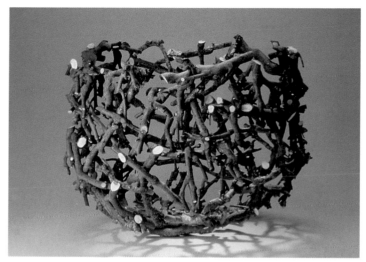

Valley House—1998
19" x 24" x 16"
plum trimmings and drywall bullets

directness of hand-building. The work presented here draws upon these basic and age-old forms of human ingenuity. The elementary technologies represented in textile structures were the precursors for many of our present day amenities, such as suspension bridges and geodesic domes, as well as computers. It is the same resourcefulness which also allows us to exploit nature. I believe that we are living in a time when our abundant skill and inventiveness has taken us to the edge of endangering the very environment which supports us.

Though, at present, some of my work incorporates wire and some welding and bronze casting, I am committed to encouraging a broader application of harvestable, endlessly renewable material in the objects of our physical culture. Concern about issues of environmental degradation fuels my creative ideas and has for many years. My work has brought to me a new appreciation for the value of things—a redefinition of what is to be kept and what is to be discarded.

Pale Weather—1994
20" x 31"
almond prunings, doweled and glued

KARI LØNNING

Inside detail: "Tall Walnut"
9" x 7¼"

All my life I knew that I would make and build things. I began college as a jewelry and metalsmithing major, but I graduated as a potter. Along the way, I studied design and became interested in weaving. But nothing clicked. Jewelry was too "tight," ceramics required too much equipment, and I was always wet and dirty, and my weaving couldn't physically stand up by itself. When I began weaving rattan baskets, everything fell into place. I could weave thrown forms and build complex constructions.

Double Darling Clementine
6" x 4¼"

Although rattan continues to offer me countless challenges, I became intrigued with a new material. Every winter I saved orange crates for some future use. The printed graphics and clean plywood motivated me to cut them up and reassemble them into open conical forms. At first, I just tied the pieces together with waxed linen. Then I glued in bases to give them strength and to maintain their shapes. As I got more involved with these vessel forms, I found myself building double-walled constructions reminiscent of the ones I wove in rattan. In addition to the patterned orange crates, now I also buy and use commercial plywoods. The lure of recycling the crates and creating classic forms has sparked my imagination. Some day, I may paint these pieces, build them larger or construct them in metal with cables. The possibilities are endless.

Clementine Series group from left to right: Mackintosh, Tall Walnut, Birch & Walnut

DONA LOOK

Although I have had informal training in various fiber arts throughout my life and received a B.A. in art from the University of Wisconsin-Oshkosh in 1970, I am a self-taught basket maker.

I choose to work with white birch bark because of the unique qualities which make it suitable for both weaving and sewing. Although I continue to collect and experiment with other materials such as cedar, basswood bark, and willow, I prefer to

#8812—1988
8½" x 11" x 11"
white birch bark and silk thread

concentrate on white birch bark. Because the quality of the bark is crucial to my work, I search out large, healthy trees that are soon to be logged. This process of gathering and preparing materials often dictates each tree's use. Technique and scale are determined by the length, thickness and elasticity of the bark. Subtle variations in proportion and color are dependent on the bark I have available. Since I begin my work in the forest, the resulting baskets may reflect my respect for these materials and my concern for the health and diversity of our northern woodlands.

Using techniques which I developed to create specific forms, I often work on a group of baskets together. Beginning with the preparation and cutting of bark for several pieces, I compare each as they evolve. They may be seen as individual pieces, but they are in fact parts of a continuous learning process.

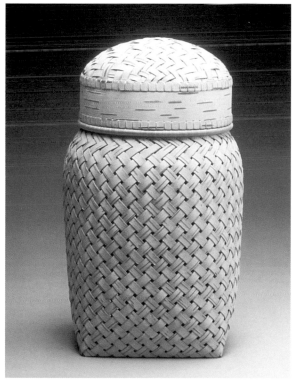

#8814—1988
10½" x 6¼" x 6¼"
white birch bark and silk thread

Although I am interested in fiber arts from other cultures and times, my ideas are influenced by environment and come from

93

memory and imagination. Innumerable fleeting images of forms seen in the past and hidden somewhere in the mind resurface by chance to be manipulated and altered by the imagination to fit the possibilities defined by the materials used. An idea may begin on the beach or in my garden, seeing the profile and volume of a pod or pumpkin. Using bark from the forest as fabric, the image is then altered to suit the materials.

I collect bark from trees that are being logged, since the stress and scars which result from peeling the bark will usually destroy the tree. There are subtle differences in the thickness and color of bark on each tree. Outer layers of bark are peeled away to provide a uniform surface. All pieces of bark are planned and cut before assembly. Side pieces are cut from the bark of one tree in order to match color and surface quality.

The top and bottom, as well as all the sides, are measured and sewn together with waxed silk thread. Edges along the side pieces are reinforced with narrow strips of bark. The top band is constructed of several layers of bark and sewn on with a hoop wrapped in waxed silk thread.

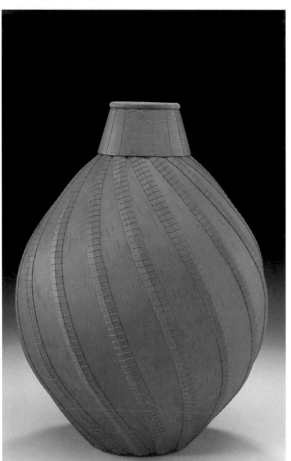

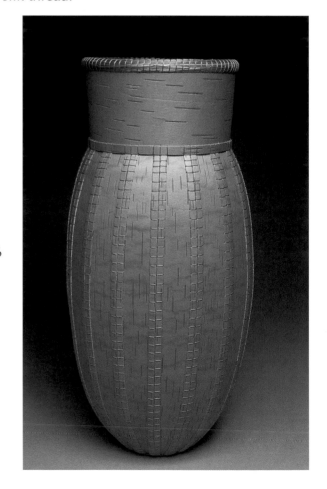

Left: #991—1999
14" x 11" x 11"
white birch bark
and silk thread

Right: #963—1996
18" x 8½" x 8½"
white birch bark
and silk thread

Photo by Johnathan Wallen

CONNIE & TOM McCOLLEY

The beginning, when do we become an artist? I think one is just born with an instinct to create. I see it in my children. We have had little formal art training. Our teacher is experience and instinct. The act of creating is the teacher and inspiration for the next basket. We were first pulled towards basketry when we moved to rural West Virginia in 1973. The process of making the white oak splints fascinated us. From the gathering of the material to the final smoothing of the wood. It was exhilarating. I love being in the woods, smelling the green, and finding those little wonders of nature that are seldom seen. Our first baskets were traditional in nature and made in the company of friends as we learned together the secrets of the wood and the weaving.

Our approach to basket making has always been quite simply to make the best baskets that we possibly can. The process is only complicated by trying to decide what "best" means. When our baskets were simple functional containers, best meant that the handles were strong and the rims substantial. It meant that they would carry whatever was put into them and would hold up to hard use. As our work has evolved into decorative objects, best meant that the colors were blended beautifully and the patterns caught the viewer's eye, leading it in a dance across the surface of the basket. Best in terms of the vessels we make today is much harder to define. But in the end our goal is to engage the spirit of the viewer and reveal to that person an aspect of our reality that may not be a part of their experience.

White oak baskets have long been prized for their durability, strength and beauty. The process begins with the careful selection of straight, young white oak trees free of twists and knots. Hand splitting of the weaving material requires time and patience to master. Each splint is then scraped to a smooth sheen, cut, dyed, then woven into a basket.

Tom prepares the rough oak to be split into individual pieces.

Green splints are preshaped before the basket "Marriage" is constructed.

We still gather all our materials. For us, it is the most important part of our work. Maybe because it takes us back to the woods, maybe because we are more in control of where the material comes from. Probably because white oak is such incredible material and you can only get it if you harvest it yourself.

The techniques we use are gathered not just from basketry. Tom uses traditional wood joinery when his treasures of twisted branches find their way into a woven form. A wood lathe is used to turn parts for others. I discovered color and with the addition of different weave patterns, added movement to our work. Some of our very favorite pieces

Along the Path—1992
25" x 36" x 20"
hickory bark and white oak

Above: Assembly—1991
12" x 23" x 21"
white oak and elm
Left: Marriage—1994
15" x 11" x 10"
white oak and sassafras

96

Over and Over Again—1988
17" x 17" x 17"
white oak

are collaborations with wood carver, Jude Binder. For many years, Jude has also been my dance teacher. The movement of body and spirit has flowed over into the baskets. The inspiration for the next piece? Could it be the few days we spent walking on the beach, a conversation with a friend, perhaps the last basket or looking back at a basket made years ago and seeing something new to try with the skills you have gathered since then.

An artist must be fearless. When you create something, you open yourself up and lay yourself out for the world to see. You cannot be afraid to fail or you would never act. You do it for yourself. It is what you are. There is an artist within each of us. We must teach ourselves, our children, to be fearless.

Above: Basket with White Oak Branch Handle—1991
16" x 25" x 22"
Right: Shell Series #7—1994
21" x 23" x 22"
white oak and cherry

Photo by Jim Osborne

John McQueen

I believe, in the beginning I wanted to make baskets because I found when I made a basket, the object I was making was the subject. If I asked what it was, the obvious answer was, it is a basket. This is different than any other art. If I am painting, I must

John working on "Haystack Lion."

Photo by Stuart Kestenbaum

being. Baskets exist because they are baskets. The object is the subject.

In time, though, their most dominant characteristic, that they are containers, began to influence my thinking. I realized the term container is very broad and my basket opened up. This pushed the definition of traditional basket making, but to me almost everything is a container. Obviously our bodies are containers, a room is a container, and almost all physical objects have an inside and an outside. I began to look at

Work in progress.

paint something. Even if it is an abstraction, the painting is not what it is physically, but is something else. It has subject matter attached to it. Sculpture is the same. It is a figure or abstract or something. What it is made from and the way it is made is not its reason for

John's studio.

objects that at first seemed either too large or long and narrow to be containers. This lead me to lakes, rivers, what I thought of as "landscape containers." However, containers do not need to be physical objects. I explored ideas such as sentences having a beginning and end and being contained within their beginning capital letter and their ending period. A concise thought is concise because it is contained. This more abstract thinking about baskets lead me to, or maybe I should say back to, the physical aspects of the basket. Literally how it was put together. If the void or hole inside it makes it a basket, I wanted to place that void or space around each element. This would move the single large inside space to many, even thousands of very small spaces throughout the structure. The result was a solid object or an object that was structurally consistent all the way through but full of many spaces.

Photo by Dave Sherwin

Above: Headstand—1997
23" x 18" x 16"
bark, plastic rivets, and string

Left: My Father Turning into a Luscombe—1998
26" x 23" x 23"
sticks and string

My question to myself was, is it still a basket if it is not a structure made up of a wall around a void, but a solid full of holes?

It seems the way I have gone about exploring these directions when it comes to actually building these objects is to use recognizable subject matter. One of these is the physical language. Making the language into objects allows me to work through some of these directions in a very real three-dimensional way, using very immediate material such as sticks and weeds. The other very recognizable object that becomes the subject matter I can hang ideas onto is the human body. Therefore, many of my pieces take the shape of the body.

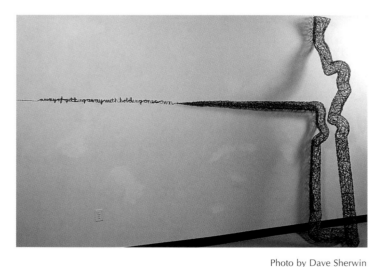

Photo by Dave Sherwin

Object Lesson (St. Joe River)—1995
7' 8" x 11' 9" x 19"
sticks and string

The Other Side of the Moon—1993
32" x 18" x 14"
bark and vine

JUDY MULFORD

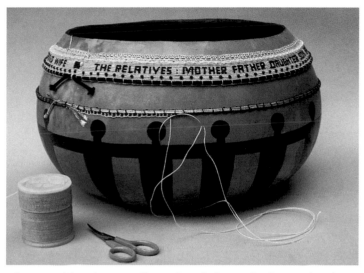

The gourd has been collected and cleaned. The top has been sawed off and the inside cleaned and painted. Holes were drilled around the top, linen was attached and the words are knotted on the surface. Paper doll designs were drawn on the gourd with permanent black marker.

Most importantly, I am a wife, mother, and "Nana" — a nurturer and a nest builder. But over 20 years ago, when I was forty, I came to a major crossroads in my life. My mothering years were over, my children were leaving the nest. Now, what would I do with the rest of my life? I decided to continue to build "nests" and call them baskets.

At first I was enamored with the materials and the fact the I could actually create a basket. I was intrigued with pine needles and spent years making semitraditional and nonfunctional pieces. Then I decided that I wanted my baskets to become something more. I wanted them to say something, to have content. I did not want to just make "sale" baskets, I wanted to make "soul" baskets that would honor and celebrate the family.

The bottom of the gourd was covered in knotless netting, using a curved needle. Pockets were added for the "babies."

Photo transfers, a shoe lace, buttons and more details were added. The base was semifinished, except for the babies.

The process was slow and scary. I realized that this creative gift was also a tool to help me work out emotional problems or passages in my life. I began using a combination of clay and pine needles, which enabled me to sculpt my own images and to make bases for my pine needle coiling. My first clay lids were of animals because they were "safe" and not controversial. Then I began to use more and more female figures that became more personal, autobiographical and graphic. I made large baskets with small figures and large figures with small baskets. The titles became important and slowly I gravitated into only making pieces that contained imagery focusing on the family, motherhood, and grandmotherhood.

The lid was made from styrofoam, coated many times with gesso and black acrylic paint and then covered with looped, black waxed linen. The five "relatives" are made with foam and polymer, covered with looping, and sewn to the basket.

By this time, my figures had become stylized and I began using waxed linen to dress them with looped, backpack pouches holding babies. I loved the looping technique and used it to cover entire clay pieces. Then it was time to take another major artistic step. I let go of my clay and pine needles and allowed myself to go forward and grow with the looping technique. For me, this versatile and ancient technique is very symbolic because it is also the buttonhole stitch which is historically rooted with woman's work in the home. Now my work is even more autobiographical, personal, graphic, and narrative. Instead of clay for this format, I use gourds, probably one of the first containers, as a base to integrate my photo images, drawings, script, and babies in pouches. The photos are from my old family album or recent family photos. Some of the buttons are antique heirlooms of my mother's or grandmother's while others have been collected at flea markets. I use silver, onyx, pearls, beads, and pounded tin can lids to

Photo by Susan Einstein

The Relatives—1999
13½" x 15"
gourd, waxed linen, photo transfers, polymer, beads, antique buttons, fine silver, Australian hematite, fresh water and cultured pearls, pounded tin can lids, paper, knotting, and looping

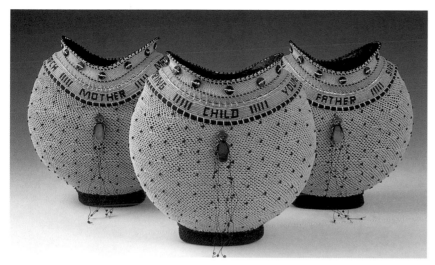

embellish these decorative vessels. I have added dolls and journals to some pieces and some dolls have become "wall dolls." The possibilities are endless. I will never run out of material.

My maternal grandmother made dolls, my mother was a loom weaver and craftsperson, and my father was a painter and sculptor. My pieces reflect the talents they have shared with me.

Above: Nana Doll—1998
11¾" x 4" x 8"

Top left: Mother-Father-Child—1998
8" x 19" x 12"

Bottom left: A Woman Is...—1998
11" x 13" x 7½"

LEON NIEHUES

I am a self-taught basket weaver and have no formal training. I was raised on a Kansas farm and credit this upbringing with my ability to set goals and work hard to accomplish them. In 1975, my wife Sharon and I moved to northwest Arkansas where there is still a tradition of craft. It was being in an environment with a craft history that made me comfortable with basketry as an occupation.

I use three materials in my baskets, white oak, coral berry runners, and waxed linen thread. I have never used any other materials, though I have experimented with a few other materials. I use these because they are readily available to me and complement each other. I look forward to gathering materials because this gets me out in the wooded areas. All this closely relates my baskets to this specific region where I live.

Basketry has been my only craft discipline. In the beginning, I made only traditional baskets with Sharon. But even these were individual with original ideas and were never production work. Now, I employ some traditional techniques along with new

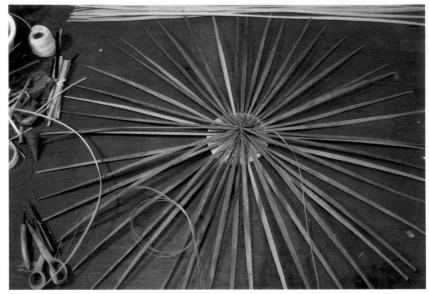

The ribs are laid out to form a double-woven round base.

Photo by Evan Niehues

Leon begins to shape the base.

104

The basket is woven out to a managable size.

Then, the basket is woven up to form a neck.

The overlay of red dyed oak ribs is temporarily stitched down to mold to the surface of the basket.

techniques that I have developed. I like to begin all my work with a solid foundation in technique and craftsmanship. Simple techniques that can be built upon are best. I look at my baskets as constructions, and I build on them until the basket is complete. The materials that I have on hand, or am able to fabricate at the time, help decide the scale I work on at any particular time.

The materials I work with are a limiting factor, but I like to work with constraints. I am comfortable with the materials I work with, they grow all around me. Before making baskets, I worked at a local sawmill and got a good education in hardwoods and a knowledge of the woods. I especially like nature and the appearance of simplicity on the surface. I try to keep my eyes open and notice what is around me. Good ideas come from everyday items that have a good sense of design. It is important to notice other craft media too. Lately, I have been looking through books on architecture and thinking about constructions that might apply to my work.

Hadassah, #27-99
24" x 13"

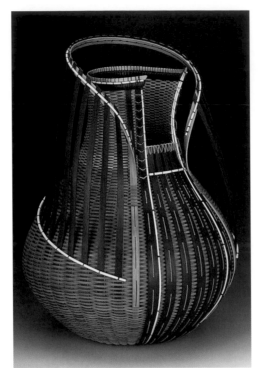

Queen Jane, #3-99
19" x 14½"

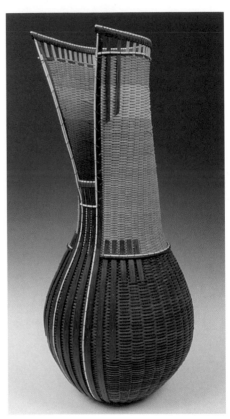

Leopold, #92-98
32½" x 14"

Right: #30-99 Cassandra
17½" x 15½"

Starting a base with Torrey pine needles.

Francina working in her studio with "company."

FRANCINA & NEIL PRINCE

"Wonder—is not precisely knowing,
and not precisely knowing not—"

Emily Dickinson

Both Fran and I were initially (and continually) attracted to the coiled fiber process by the repetitive rhythmic sequence utilizing locally abundant natural fibers. The vessel form, with its inner space protected by a thin walled outer surface, suggested seemingly endless variations in form, pattern, and color.

Construction from many individual natural elements in which structure defines decoration aptly satisfies our creative impulse. This pure structural simplicity is described by the helix, a universal mathematical principle underlying galaxies, as well as DNA. A basket created from a continuous helical coil of fibers represents a personal crystallization of space and time. Surprise, whether elation or disappointment, always awaits the completed work.

The sense of place, and renewal of the seasons learned from yearly gathering and harvesting shape our way of life. To create positive expressions with one's life energy is a joyful enterprise. I now see basketry as a metaphor for discipline and order in our lives during these chaotic times.

Note: *The preceding text was prepared for exhibition of the permanent collection of contemporary American baskets Curator Jack Lenor Larsen, Erie Art Museum, August 1988.*

I work with a rare species of pine growing in sheltered places about the coastal bluffs in southern California. After a three-year life attached to the tree, Torrey pine needles are brought to earth by desert-born Santa Ana winds. Collecting bags of fallen needles annually allows me the opportunity of harvesting nature's processes.

Showing how bundles of pine needle are coiled.

Creating a vessel from a continuous unbroken coil of pine needles puts me in touch with:

place & work, life & art
The Torrey pine, a relic of the Ice Age connects me to
The Tree of Life

Historians believed that European mariners who began charting the California coast in the 16th century used the distinctive Torrey pine-topped sea cliffs called "Punta de los Arboles" (Point of Trees) as a navigational aid. The Pines continued to be a confirmed sailors' landmark well into the 19th century.

Before the territory of California achieved full statehood in 1850, physician-naturalist Charles Parry made a botanical find of a unique pine with distorted branches and clusters of long terminal leaves. He named the tree "Pinus Torreyana" tributing his mentor eminent American botanist John Torrey.

To secure this unusual and rare conifer from extinction, local authorities through the years have stimulated aggressive guardianship and safeguards to continue this species.

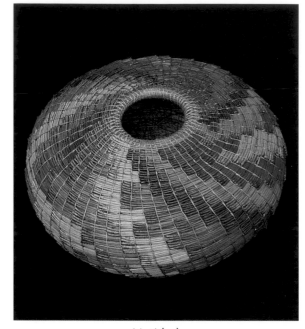

Untitled
10" x 17"
Torrey pine needles

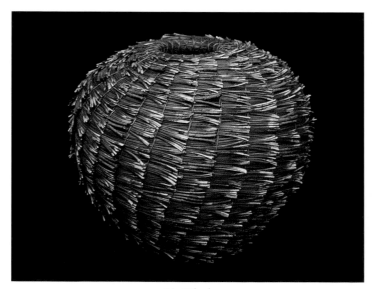

Untitled
10" x 9"
Torrey pine needles

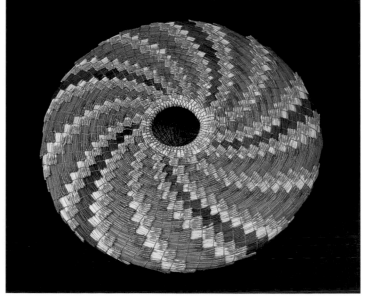

Untitled
8" x 17"
Torrey pine needles

Photo by Gerry Biron

Photo by Gerry Biron

JoAnne Russo

Baskets have always fascinated me. They seemed so complex; I wondered how they were made. It was not until 1984, while living in York, Maine, that I wove my first reed basket from a kit. I was intrigued not only with making baskets, but learning their history. Long ago a community living in the Mount Agamenticus area of York eked out a living making ash baskets. I went to the historical society to find examples of their work and eventually wound up giving a basket-making demonstration, where I met Raymond Weare. He had learned how to use white ash from the last of the Agamenticus basket makers and was glad to share his knowledge with me. Now, not only did I know how to make baskets, I learned to process the raw materials.

It is not easy work. It is important to use green wood and keep the log from drying out. I usually roll a log I am not working on in a plastic tarp and keep in under a shed. When using white ash, we make billets, which are long, narrow widths, many growth rings thick. To do this, we would keep splitting an eight-foot log until we had narrow pie-shaped wedges. Using a drawknife, these wedges were squared off to form a uniform width and thickness, usually 1" x 2"–3". We then pounded these sticks to separate the growth rings. My first white ash basket was a large backpack that I used to carry supplies to basket classes I was teaching at the local high school.

Now that I use black ash, I work the entire log. I take the bark off then pound it with a sledgehammer to separate the growth rings. These pull off the tree in narrow strips the length of the log and are

Top: JoAnne works on one basket as another one waits its turn.

Center: After completing a row around a basket, JoAnne goes over it again with dyed ash, making the porcupine curlicues.

Bottom: Pine needles are sewn over the rim with nylon thread.

removed, layer by layer, all the way to the heartwood. The splints can dry out or be worked on right away. I sort through the pile, saving the very thick ones for rims and splitting others into thinner strips. The splitting process reveals the shiny, satin-like inside of the growth ring. Then the outer side is scraped and pulled through cutters to produce the different widths I use for weaving.

My first baskets were functional, utilitarian and free-form. I found myself continually backtracking, ripping out rows to get the shape back in symmetry. That is

Photo by Jeff Baird

Black Porcupine—1998
8" x 8"
black ash, pine needles, and porcupine quills

Photo by Jeff Baird

Porcupine—1996
11" x 10"
black ash, pine needles, and porcupine quills

when I started to weave over basket molds. Now I draw the designs on paper and my husband turns out a wooden form on a lathe. I weave the basket over this mold which has been cut into nine pieces and is held together with Velcro. Once the weaving is complete, I pull out the middle section, then reach in and take out the rest of the pieces. The mold can be put back together to use again. Working this way allows me to create twill patterns as I weave or concentrate on making the "porcupine" curlicues line up precisely around the basket. What some would think of as "tedious," I find very meditative.

I work on many pieces at once, doing a few rows on some, starting new ones and finishing others. Most of my baskets start out narrow at the base, get wider and then narrow again. The ash is slightly wet as I weave so it expands and shrinks back to its original width when dry, leaving small gaps between the rows. I weave a few rows, then let it dry overnight. The next day, before continuing, I push the rows back down to tighten them up. This start and stop process continues until I have enough rows to take the mold out of the basket. Once out, it will sit for a few days before tucking spokes and finishing the rim.

When people see my baskets for the first time, they remark on how detailed and precise they are. It seems second nature for me to work this way. I remember watching my mother and grandmother knitting and crocheting sweaters, mittens, and afghans. My grandmother taught me how to crochet before I could read. All my stuffed dogs were outfitted in sweaters and hats and all the shades in our house had intricate pulls I had crocheted out of string. While in grade school, I was taught how to sew. My aunt showed me how to cut out patterns, measure precisely, and sew with the skill of a tailor. She instilled in me the patience to do the job right; mistakes were ripped out and done again.

Before I started making baskets, I collected both antique and contemporary ones from the Indian tribes in Maine. Made to sell to tourists, they were called fancy baskets as they were detailed with dyed ash, twisted into curlicues. Many were in the shapes of strawberries, blueberries, and ears of corn and dyed accordingly. Through the use of the curlicue and other embellishments, they transformed the utilitarian basket into an object d'art. In my work, I try to integrate the traditional form into a contemporary object to create a basket that has the feel of being both old and new.

Photo by Jeff Baird

Double Basket—1999
7" x 8"
black ash and pine needles

Jester—1997
39" x 11" x 11"
paper twine, wood, wire cloth, brass wire, brass
pins, and mixed polymers

DEBRA M. SACHS

An object can be so thoughtfully designed, it evokes the spiritual without direct reference to content. The design, itself, is the content. This is what I aim to accomplish in the objects I make. The design includes fabricating objects, mostly out of wood and metal, combining building and basketry techniques. It also includes the use of other materials, such as tiny glass or steel balls, wire, paint, and polymers, to manipulate the surfaces. Object design (the shape of an object) and surface design are the two elements I combine to create a unique sculpture.

The materials I use are generally industrial. The wood is construction lumber, deliberately chosen for its innate imperfections. The inconsistent grain creates subtle but unusual surface patterns. Copper refrigeration tube has also been prominent in my work for many years. This common plumbing material lends itself beautifully to be coiled and woven. Brass tubes are the spokes around which the copper tube is woven. Paper twine (commonly used for the handles of paper bags) is also used for weaving. Pins, nails, staples, washers, any of these materials might simultaneously serve a decorative and functional purpose in my work.

The goal is to create an object that is its own unique being in the world. This object projects a personality. This personality is created through a variety of design elements. These design elements are integrated into a whole. This whole is a being whose sum is far greater than its parts.

Left: Spotted Pod—
1998–1999
68" x 16" x 16"
wood, copper
tube, copper wire,
copper tacks, and
polymers

Right: Purple
Pod—1997
30" x 12" x 12"
wood, copper
tube, paper twine,
copper wire, and
mixed polymers

JANE SAUER

I love the sense of building, knot by knot and row by row. I think of the rows of knots as lines wrapping around a form, giving it movement, weight, and direction. I love making order from the chaos of hundreds of threads and thousands of knots. For me, the repetitiveness of the process is rhythmic and meditative. The boundaries of form and color seem to be endless and each piece stimulates numerous ideas for the next piece of work. Yet the most essential element is always the potential of this technique and material to be used as a dialogue between myself and the viewer.

My shapes have become progressively simpler and more sculptural as I have become increasingly more interested in the message of my work and less self-conscious about the technical aspects of the making. I seek to create forms that speak to the viewer, and challenge or provoke thoughts or emotions. I use subtle veils and washes of color to further project my concepts. Most recently, I have been intrigued by relationships, both global and personal. Many of my works consist of two or three parts placed in a specific relationship to each other. The empty space between

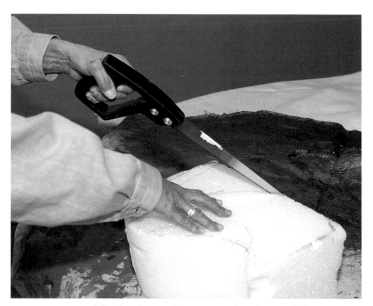

Jane carves a block of styrofoam into the desired shape.

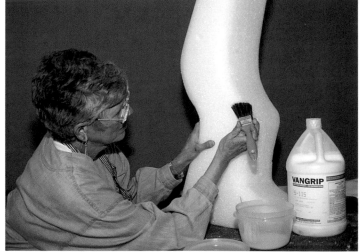

Four to five coats of polymer or gesso are applied to the styrofoam to act as a barrier between the foam and the threads.

114

each piece is as important as the positive space. I want the whole to be stronger than each part. I select shapes and gestures which express circumstances, tensions, contradictions, and the interplay of relationships in life.

Above: Lark's head knots are added to the core to form the beginning circle. Knotting begins by pulling the two ends of the core thread. As additional threads are needed, new lark's head knots are added to the core.

Threads are painted prior to knotting or during the knotting process. Acrylic paint mixed with about one third mat medium is used. A small amount of water is added depending on the desired consistency.

Below: Jane knots up the side of the styrofoam piece.

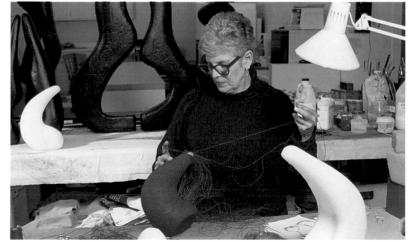

Left: Protection & Other Domestic Stories
37" x 14½" x 12½"
waxed linen, thread, and paint

Right: No Separation—1998
27½" x 16" x 10"
waxed linen, thread, and paint

Hisako Sekijima

I define a basket as an object, often a vessel shape created in a textile structure, where the dynamics of each component are visible. My expanded definition includes anything implying a relationship to basketry in its technical, aesthetic, or functional terms. To me, that vocabulary includes: Lines bending, looping, passing under, over, crossing; resilience; flexibility; self-supporting, standing, rigid; planes folding, bending, layering to obtain volume; drawing lines in space, filling space; eliminating material to form space into parts; accumulating spaces into a large whole; package, trapping or wrapping space; enclosing, containing; shifting dimensions; repetition, rhythm, texture, pattern; order, disorder, joining, connecting, binding; disassembling, screening, enhancing; curiosity; sphere, binding around, bundling; handle, carrying; hanging, pressing, weighing balancing; cutting, peeling, piercing; breaking, unweaving, making holes.

I studied the basics of rattan basket making with a rattan furniture maker, Akimichi Hashimoto, in Japan in the early 1970s. I prefer crude materials, because they give me more problems. They offer me greater challenges to think. I enjoy a vivid contact with

Above Left: "Fittings II" in the beginning stages.

Left: "Fittings II" in progress.

nature's domain in my effort to match my reality with natures rules. I do not simply regard the so-called "basketry techniques" as ways of making, but rather as an abstract essence of structure.

I prefer crude materials. I work with plant materials collected by myself from my vicinity, wherever I live: in suburban towns or central Tokyo. I am preoccupied with space, textuality, structural surface, and architectural quality. I think form reveals richer aspects when it is viewed not only in terms of the real materials such as sticks or bark, but in terms of space or holes in which real material is not present. The matter of basket structure might seem to deal only with material or technical domain, which is not relevant to me. But I now know that structural interplay of the material's property and constructing method works creatively only when I personally become conscious of its nature, merits, and limits. It is dependent on how I see and think. The finished object reveals clearly how I have changed from what I was before I made the piece.

I call myself a basket maker because I inform my work

#392 Fittings—1992
13" x 9⅞" x 8¼"
cherry and maple

by thinking and processing the nature and history of basketry. And also, because in order to realize the ideas, I choose to use materials and structural methods that have typically been used for basket making. It pleases me that my ideas and the final results of my work expand the boundary well beyond what I once thought of as the domain of basketry.

#433 Resilience V—1997
4" x 21" x 21"
looped willow

#394 Untitled Basket—1994
7½" x 14½" x 14½"
randomly interlaced bamboo

Kay Sekimachi

In much of my work I have been interested in the see-through object—the overlapping of translucent planes as in my woven monofilament hangings, and in my paper bowls, the overlayering of sheer pieces of paper. I always hope my work looks and feels "right," that my use of material is sensitive and honest and works with the technique and form.

Note: *The preceding text was prepared for Brown/Grotta Gallery, The 10th Wave, Part 4, New Baskets and Freestanding Fiber Sclupture, April 1997.*

The leaves, kiriwood paper, and handmade paper called washi are themselves the source of my inspiration. Other materials I have worked with include hornet's nest paper, skeleton leaves, and hand-woven fabrics.

Though subconscious, my Japanese heritage is reflected in my aesthetics. I have chosen to work in neutral tones because I want people to see the forms before being distracted by their use of color. I have tried to develop a way of working where the materials and techniques can speak for themselves.

Asian Willow I—1998
7" x 6"
skeleton of leaves,
paper watercolor, and
wallpaper paste

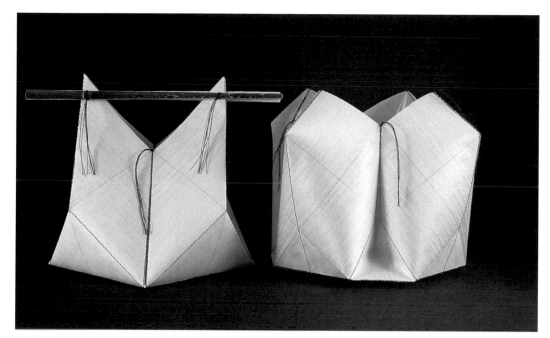

Kiri I and Kiri II—1993
7" x 7" x 7" each
folded and stitched
kiriwood paper

Photo by Carley Fonville

Washi Vessels—1993
15" x 8" x 8" and
12½" x 8" x 8"
folded and stitched antique
Japanese paper, indigo-dyed
and persimmon tannin

Photo by Charles Frizzell

KARYL SISSON

In college I was an art major studying painting and drawing. After graduating, I earned money doing commercial art while making my own art on the side. Influenced by the soft sculptures of Oldenburg and the burgeoning fiber movement in the 70s, I began to make three-dimensional wall art with old fabrics and buttons. Eventually, the work left the wall.

In the 70s, I developed an obsession for collecting—particularly sewing notions and assorted sundries from the 50s and 60s that relate to domesticity and the feminine persona. These collectibles either find their way into my work (which is a good thing since I am running out of storage space), or serve as inspiration. I like the idea of recycling materials and working with objects that have a history.

I have always been interested in vernacular architecture and how indigenous cultures use materials at hand to create structure. So it seemed only natural that basketry

Left: An adjustable frame with rayon military tape is shown. The warp and weft are attached to the frame with push pins.

Right: Karyl demonstrates the wrapped, twining technique.

Photo by Susan Einstein

Photo by Susan Einstein

122

books would provide a clue for how to interlock many of my collected materials. The form, patterning, and texture of my sculptures are an intrinsic expression of the basketry techniques I use. But it is not the basketry skills that are of primary importance to me, although I do appreciate the process (even as I curse its lack of immediacy). I am interested mostly in the physical possibilities of the materials and the tactile and suggestive qualities of the form.

I see my work as sculpture. However, not acknowledging its textile heritage denies its rich history, and to view it strictly as craft denies its roots (and mine) in the fine arts. One discipline need not exclude the other.

Left: The weft ends are stitched up to form a big pocket.

Right: Dyed miniature clothespins are clipped on. This piece uses approximately 1,800 clothespins.

Photo by M. Liszt

Photo by M. Liszt

123

W/arp—1999
14" x 12" x 14"
rayon military tape, thread,
and miniature, spring-
operated, wooden
clothespins

Below: Hip—1997
13" x 11" x 13"
cotton twill tape, thread,
and miniature, spring-
operated, wooden
clothespins

Photo by Susan Einstein

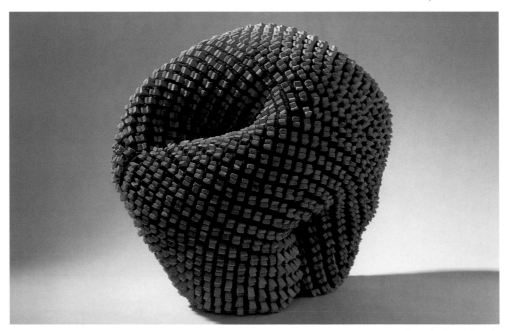

Photo by Susan Einstein

Opening Up—1997
13½" x 27" x 20"
cotton twill tape, thread, and
spring-operated, wooden
clothespins

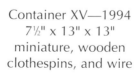

Container XV—1994
7½" x 13" x 13"
miniature, wooden
clothespins, and wire

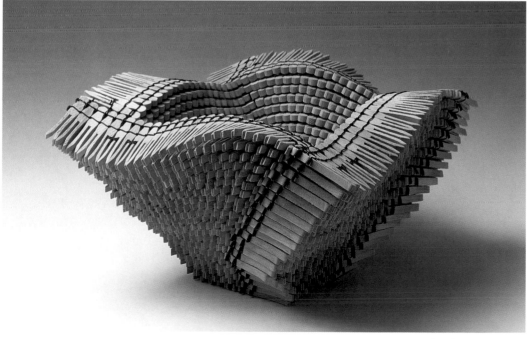

JIRO YONEZAWA

Jiro slices bamboo strips and separates the outer layer of the bamboo from the inner layer, which is not used.

The bamboo strips are trimmed to make an even width.

When I was 22, I spent a year traveling around Southeast Asia and was struck by the myriad of uses for baskets. I was reminded of how bamboo baskets and containers were widely used in Japan when I was a child. After I returned to Japan, I learned bamboo basketry. The abundance of bamboo in my surroundings and its availability to create things to use in daily life was appealing. As I began to study, I met many bamboo artists and began to realize the potential of the material and the scope of techniques and form. The techniques of preparing bamboo, weaving techniques, and finishing techniques (including the use of dyes and urushi lacquer) were all included in my training.

However, after I finished two years of training and an apprenticeship with Masakatsu Ono, I decided not to pursue basketry as a vocation. I spent the next five years farming. In 1989, our family moved to the United States and I considered basketry again. I began by using local materials such as black bamboo, sea grass, and pine. The pieces were similar to work that I learned in Japan. I gradually started to make larger pieces.

Now I use cured mandake bamboo, which I import from Japan. The hardness, durability, and surface quality are all excellent. I appreciate its flexibility and texture as a woven material. It is the material I was trained to use and I am still exploring its potential. I dye my materials with commercial dyes. The most important step in finishing my work is the application of urushi lacquer.

I often use cedar root, which the Native Americans here also use, for surface decoration. It is abundant, flexible, and strong and its character works well with the style of baskets I make. Sometimes I use split ash. I like the structure and strength. I also use cane for wrapping the rims and occasionally for surface decoration. This is also imported from Asia. Recently, I have been exploring the use of steel and brass in some of my work. I feel a responsibility to use materials to create work that will last well beyond my lifetime.

As an apprentice in Japan, I learned the importance of attention to detail and the depth of technique. I am always trying to improve my technique and explore the potential of form and material. I mostly use the twill weave and try to capture various forms with the weave. I use traditional weaving techniques, but have developed original construction techniques. Depending on the materials used, I consider the balance of shape, texture, color, and surface finish. Much thought is given to the outward appearance, but the inside is just as important.

Through a serious study of traditional techniques, one can create work which is contemporary and original. Refining one's skill as a craftsman is an important part of creating art.

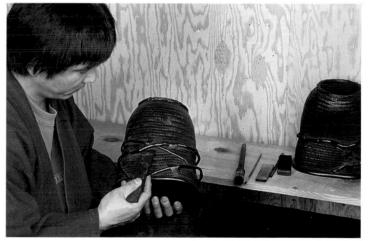

Jiro weaves the body of the basket. This basket will later be fitted into a wooden base.

Urushi lacquer is applied with a brush. The lacquer will then be dried in a dryer and then another layer of lacquer will be applied. Sometimes Jiro sprinkles on a fine powder of soot and other ingredients after two or three coats. Depending on the basket and the desired finish, three to seven coats of lacquer are applied. After the piece is lacquered, Jiro polishes it with a wax made from insects.

Mutation—1998
13" x 35" x 8"
bamboo, cane, cedar root, wood, and urushi lacquer

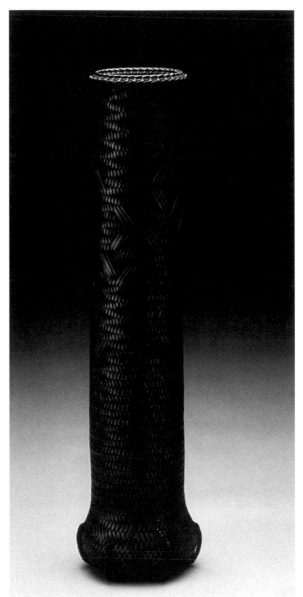

Left: Noble Soul—
1999
9½" x 9"
bamboo, cane,
cedar root, wood
and urushi lacquer

Right: Tera—1994
22" x 5½"
bamboo, cane, and
urushi lacquer

SELECTED RESOURCES

We would like to offer our sincere appreciation of the valuable support given in this ever-changing industry of new ideas, concepts, designs, and products. Several projects shown in this publication were created with the outstanding and innovative products developed by:

H. H. Perkins (reed supplier)
10 S. Bradley Rd.
Woodbridge, CT 06525
800-462-6660
www.hhperkins.com

Allen's Basketworks
P. O. Box 3217
Palm Springs, CA 92263
800-284-7333
www.allensbasketworks.com

PRO Chemical & Dye
P. O. Box 14
Somerset, MA 02726
800-228-9393
www.prochemical.com

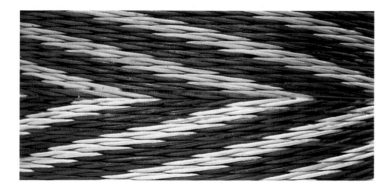 

RECOMMENDED READING

For further information on using round reed and basket making, I recommend the following reading:

The Basketmakers Art, Contemporary Baskets and Their Makers, Lark Books, 1986, ISBN 0 937274 28 3

Basketry, Projects from Baskets to Grass Slippers, Hisako Sekijima, Kodansha International Ltd. 1986, ISBN 0 87011 751 3

Baskets as Textile Art, Ed Rossbach, Van Rostrand Reinhold Co., 1973, ISBN 0 442 27049 6

Contemporary International Basketmaking, Mary Butcher in association with the Crafts Council, Merrill Holberton, 1999, ISBN 1 85894 078 8

Contemporary Wicker Basketry, Flo Hoppe, Lark Books, 1996, ISBN 1 887 374 159

How to Wrap 5 Eggs, Hideyuki Oka Harper & Row, 1967

Interlacing, The Elemental Fabric, Jack Lenor Larsen, Kodansha International, 1979, ISBN 0 87011 778 5

METRIC CONVERSION TABLES

cm—Centimetres
Inches to Centimetres

inches	cm	inches	cm
⅛	0.3	20	50.8
¼	0.6	21	53.3
½	1.3	22	55.9
⅝	1.6	23	58.4
¾	1.9	24	61.0
⅞	2.2	25	63.5
1	2.5	26	66.0
1¼	3.2	27	68.6
1½	3.8	28	71.1
1¾	4.4	29	73.7
2	5.1	30	76.2
2½	6.4	31	78.7
3	7.6	33	83.8
3½	8.9	34	86.4
4	10.2	35	88.9
4½	11.4	36	91.4
5	12.7	37	94.0
6	15.2	38	96.5
7	17.8	39	99.1
8	20.3	40	101.6
9	22.9	41	104.1
10	25.4	42	106.7
11	27.9	43	109.2
12	30.5	44	111.8
13	33.0	45	114.3
14	35.6	46	116.8
15	38.1	47	119.4
16	40.6	48	121.9
17	43.2	49	124.5
18	45.7	50	127.0
19	48.3		

oz. - Ounces
g. - Grams
16 oz. = 1 lb.
Lbs. - Pounds
Kg. - Kilograms
1,000 g. = 1 Kg.

Solid Measures
Ounces to Grams & Pounds to Kilograms

oz.	g.	Lbs.	Kg.
1	28.35	1	.4536
2	56.7	2	.907
3	85.05	3	1.361
4	113.4	4	1.814
5	141.75	5	2.268
6	170.1	6	2.722
7	198.45	7	3.175
8	226.8	8	3.629
9	255.15	9	4.082
10	283.5	10	4.536
11	311.85	11	4.99
12	340.2	12	5.443
13	368.55	13	5.897
14	396.9	14	6.350
15	425.25	15	6.804

ACKNOWLEDGMENTS

Photo by Shel Secunda

I want to thank the 23 artists who agreed to work with me on this project. Receiving their slides and statements felt like Christmas. Talking to them reminded me that I am part of something bigger than just my studio and gardens. What most of them didn't know was how much they bolstered my energy and enthusiasm as I waded through all the paperwork.

Thank you also to my sister Lucy, who lent me her hands, her copier, and her patience. And to Donna, who always made time for my emergency help calls.

Thank you to browngrotta arts for representing and supporting so many of us. And to the rest of my family and friends who patiently stuck by me as I wondered why a three-dimensional artist would ever agree to write a book.

Finally to Barneby, my best friend and love, for keeping everything in proper perspective. He made me take walks to get away from writing — every day, whether I felt like it or not. Life is simple, as long as he can go swimming and retrieve tennis balls, life is good.

INDEX